UNDERSTANDING PUBLIC LAW

Gabriele Ganz is Emeritus Professor of Law at the
University of Southampton

UNDERSTANDING LAW
Editor: J.A.G. Griffith

Understanding Law
John N. Adams and Roger Brownsword

Understanding Contract Law
John N. Adams and Roger Brownsword

Understanding Criminal Law
C.M.V. Clarkson

Understanding Public Law
Gabriele Ganz

Understanding Equity and Trusts
Jeffrey Hackney

Understanding Tort Law
Carol Harlow

Understanding Property Law
W.T. Murphy and Simon Roberts

Gabriele Ganz

UNDERSTANDING PUBLIC LAW

Third Edition

LONDON
SWEET & MAXWELL
2001

Third Edition published by Sweet & Maxwell Ltd
of 100 Avenue Road, Swiss Cottage, London NW3 3PF
(http://www.sweetandmaxwell.co.uk)

Second Edition published by Fontana Press 1994
First Edition published by Fontana Press 1987

ISBN 0421 635 703

Typeset by J&L Composition Ltd, Filey, North Yorkshire

Printed in England by
MPG Books Ltd, Bodmin, Cornwall

CONTENTS

INTRODUCTION TO THE THIRD EDITION

The preparation of this edition has been a daunting task. The Labour government elected in 1997 has propagated constitutional change on an unprecedented scale. The radical programme of constitutional reform agreed with the Liberal Democrats before the election was implemented with relentless speed. Manifesto pledges on the reform of the House of Lords, devolution, human rights and freedom of information have been honoured, though not always in the way envisaged by its supporters. The pledge which is still in abeyance is to hold a referendum on a system of proportional representation for the election of the U.K. Parliament.

But in addition to these fundamental constitutional reforms hardly an institution or procedure has escaped modernisation. These include the House of Commons, the civil service, local government, tribunals and inquiries, the Ombudsman system, the civil and criminal justice system, judicial review, the Bank of England, export licensing, surveillance and interception of communications, the police complaints system and the law relating to terrorism. This list is by no means exhaustive and does not include changes in the European Union or Northern Ireland or in substantive policy areas such as social security, education or the NHS, where fundamental reforms have been undertaken. Over 300 task forces have been set up and the legislative programme stretched to breaking point.

The only institution which has not been modernised is the Crown, though the monarchy has been the subject of much discussion and criticism especially since the death of Princess Diana in a car crash in Paris in 1997. In particular the Act of Settlement 1701, which bars anyone who is a Roman Catholic or marries a Roman Catholic from succeeding to the Crown, has come under attack and a resolution to remove this bar was passed in the Scottish Parliament (December 16, 1999) and debated in the House of Lords. There has also been much discussion of the advantages and disadvantages of a republic (*The Guardian*, December 6, 2000) but a referendum in Australia on replacing the monarch by a

President as Head of State was defeated (November 6, 1999). There have been no changes to the powers which are exercised in the name of the Crown by the government enabling it to wield substantial power without the approval of Parliament (Chapter 3).

Never has it been more true to say that describing the constitution is like trying to hit a moving target (Introduction to the First Edition). The alterations made for this edition had to be updated several times and the target is still moving. But the end of the second millennium is a suitable completion date with an early general election in 2001, which is likely to bring further constitutional changes.

At the time of the first edition almost every aspect of the constitution was under attack; at the time of the second edition the outlook for constitutional reform was bleak. Now we have had a plethora, if not a surfeit, of constitutional reform but this has not stilled criticism not only by opponents but by the Government's supporters. This may be the inevitable result of the impossibility of pleasing everyone but it is also an indication that the reforms have been driven through Parliament, often under a timetable, by a government with a huge majority rather than reached by consensus resulting from negotiation. The latter may be more lasting but the former is in the tradition of adversarial politics reflected in the electoral system, which is the linchpin of our representative democracy.

1
ELECTIVE DICTATORSHIP

The extent to which the perception of the British constitution has changed over the last hundred years is well illustrated by quotations from Dicey's *Law of the Constitution* (1885) and Lord Hailsham's lecture "Elective Dictatorship" (1976). First, Dicey on sovereignty: "The essential property of representative government is to produce coincidence between the wishes of the sovereign and the wishes of the subjects ... This, which is true in its nature of all real representative government, applies with special truth to the English House of Commons" (p. 84). On conventions, Dicey said: "The conventions of the constitution now consist of customs which (whatever their historical origin) are at the present day maintained for the sake of ensuring the supremacy of the House of Commons and, ultimately, through the elective House of Commons, of the nation" (pp. 430–31). Contrast these quotations with Lord Hailsham: "So the sovereignty of Parliament has increasingly become, in practice, the sovereignty of the Commons, and the sovereignty of the Commons has increasingly become the sovereignty of the government, which in addition to its influence in Parliament, controls the party whips, the party machine and the civil service. This means that what has always been an elective dictatorship in theory, but one in which the component parts operated, in practice, to control one another, has become a machine in which one of those parts has come to exercise a predominant influence over the rest" (p. 497). And more succinctly: "The government controls Parliament and not Parliament the government" (p. 496). So the nub of the indictment is that the elected part of Parliament, namely the House of Commons, having achieved supremacy over the unelected parts, namely the Queen and the House of Lords, has surrendered its sovereignty to the government which controls it through the party machine.

Which of these snapshots represents a more accurate picture of the constitution as it exists today? If the aim of representative government is "to produce coincidence between the wishes of the sovereign and the wishes of the subjects" the representative body must reflect the wishes of the electorate and exercise control over the government. The crucial issues, therefore, are the electoral system and the relationship between the government and Parliament.

ELECTORAL SYSTEM

Historically the electoral system is based on the representation of communities. This is still reflected in the qualification for voting and the method of voting. Everyone who is 18, a Commonwealth citizen (who is legally in the U.K.) or a citizen of Eire, not a peer who is entitled to sit in the House of Lords (see below Chapter 2) and not serving a sentence of imprisonment or held in a mental institution as a consequence of criminal activity is entitled to be placed on the electoral register in a constituency where he is resident. Residence does not now involve a qualifying period or residence on a particular date (formerly October 10). It may not even now require a degree of permanence, which was sufficiently manifested by the women protesting at Greenham Common (*Hipperson v. Newbury Electoral Registration Officer*, 1985). A person can be resident where he is staying at a place otherwise than on a permanent basis if he has no home elsewhere (Representation of the People Act 2000, s.3). This could apply, for example, to travellers. Similarly, a homeless person, who is not resident at any address, can be registered if he gives an address of a place where he spends a substantial part of his time. Patients in mental hospitals, other than those detained there for criminal activity, can now be treated as resident at the mental hospital and those remanded in custody, who have not been convicted of an offence, can be treated as resident at the place of detention. Those who cannot satisfy the residence qualification may be entitled to be registered in a constituency where they were resident, *e.g.* if they are absent because they are members of the armed forces or British citizens living abroad who have been registered there within the preceding 20 years (Representation of the People Act 1989). In such cases entitlement to vote is based on citizenship rather than residence to which lip-service is paid through registration in the constituency where the citizen was previously resident. Such a notional residence is essential as all voters must be on an electoral roll in a constituency.

The constituency is the linchpin of our electoral system. Its origin lies in the representation of communities which is still an important part of an M.P.'s work. There is, however, a constant tension between this concept of representation and the modern party system which affects so many facets of our representative democracy. It manifests itself at the outset when the constituency boundaries are drawn. These are now reviewed every eight to twelve years (Boundary Commissions Act 1992) by four politically impartial Boundary Commissions, one for each part of the United Kingdom (Parliamentary Constituencies Act 1986). Their functions will be taken over in due course by the Electoral Commission set up under the Political Parties, Elections and Referendums Act 2000. Their terms of reference enjoin them to create constituencies as near as possible to the electoral quota which is obtained by dividing the electorate of that part of the United Kingdom by the number of constituencies in it without crossing county or London borough boundaries (unless there are exceptional circumstances) and taking into account local ties. The number of seats has increased with each review and is now 659 but the changes in population are not evenly spread throughout the country. This has profound implications for the political parties but political considerations cannot be taken into account by the Commissions and, therefore, political arguments are put to them cloaked in arguments about local ties (Home Affairs Committee Report, H.C. 97 (1986–87), p. 80). Not surprisingly nearly every review since 1945 has given rise to political controversy. In 1969 the Labour government refused to implement the Boundary Commissions' recommendations and in 1983 unsuccessfully challenged them in Court (*R. v. Boundary Commission for England ex parte Foot*, 1983).

The crucial importance of constituency boundaries to the outcome of elections is the result of our electoral system, called first past the post, under which an M.P. is elected for a constituency if he receives one vote more than his nearest rival however small his percentage of the total vote. This not only enables M.P.s to be elected on a minority vote (312 M.P.s in 1997) but on two occasions since the war (1951 and February 1974) the party gaining most seats polled fewer votes than the main opposition party. Most disadvantaged by our electoral system are the Liberal Democrats, whose support is fairly evenly spread throughout the country and who come second in a large number of seats but only win a handful of seats where their support is concentrated. In 1997 they gained 46 seats for 17 per cent of the vote, whilst Labour gained 418 seats for 43 per cent and the Conservatives 165 seats with 31 per cent of the vote. It is this glaring discrepancy between seats and votes since the revival of the Liberal party in 1974 which has fuelled the pressure for electoral reform. The result of the 2001 election has left this situation virtually unchanged.

As these figures illustrate the system can also be unfair to the major parties. Labour obtained over 60 per cent of the seats with 43 per cent of the vote whilst the Conservatives gained 25 per cent of the seats with 31 per cent of the vote. Even more startling is that Labour polled fewer votes in 1997 (13.5 million) than the Conservatives in 1992 (14 million) and achieved an overall majority of 179 seats, whereas the Conservatives only managed a majority of 21 in 1992. There were several reasons for this. The turnout of voters was much lower in 1997 (only 71.5 per cent against 77.7 per cent in 1992) and some of the lowest polls were in Labour seats. Liberal Democrat voters switched to Labour in greater numbers than to Conservatives. Most importantly the election was won in approximately 100 seats where the lowest swing of votes was needed to win the seat. By targeting these seats Labour achieved better than average results where they counted most. Election campaigns have, therefore, become highly professional operations focused on a narrow band of voters, who are canvassed and cajoled, often at the expense of the party's traditional supporters. The 2001 election with a record low turnout of 59 per cent confirmed these trends.

The concentration on these marginal seats highlights the importance of constituency boundaries and their review by the Boundary Commissions. These reviews have to reflect the movement of population from the North to the South and out of the cities to the rural hinterland. This has traditionally been unfavourable to the Labour party but at the latest review Labour was able to avoid the worst effects by skilful presentations to the Commissions. Such deleterious effects as remained were more than neutralised by the 10 per cent swing against the Conservatives and the factors discussed above which were weighted against the Conservatives.

In fulfilment of a pre-election agreement with the Liberal Democrats, which was embodied in its manifesto, Labour set up a Commission under the chairmanship of Lord Jenkins, a leading Liberal Democrat peer and former Labour Minister, to recommend the best alternative system to the existing system of voting. They thus became the first government elected triumphantly under the present system to set in train the process of reform. Whether the choice between the existing system and an alternative system is put to the electorate in a referendum after the 2001 election remains to be seen.

The fairness of an electoral system must be judged not only by the proportionality of votes to seats but by the proportionality of power. If seats had been allocated in proportion to votes in

Britain, the third party (now the Liberal Democrats) would have held the balance of power since 1974, as its counterpart did in Germany for 30 years. This gives disproportionate power to a minority party. The Jenkins Commission was asked to take into account both proportionality of votes and stable government (which is not the hall-mark of coalitions) as well as the link between an M.P. and a geographical constituency.

The Commission in its report (Cm 4090, 1998) rejected the Alternative Vote which retains single member constituencies but where voters list candidates in order of preference and which ensures that an M.P. is elected by more than 50 per cent of the votes including second-preference votes. One of its main reasons was that it would have disadvantaged the Conservatives in 1997 disproportionately because of the strength of the anti-Conservative vote. It also rejected the Single Transferable Vote, where votes are cast for candidates in order of preference in multi-member constituencies and seats are allocated according to a complicated formula, partly because of its complexity. It came down in favour of a version of the Additional Member System used in Germany, where a proportion of M.P.s are elected in single member constituencies and these are then topped-up by M.P.s elected from a party list so as to achieve proportionality — each voter having two votes, one for a constituency M.P. and one for the party. The constituency M.P. would be elected by the Alternative Vote system. For the top-up M.P.s Britain would be divided into 80 areas returning one or two M.P.s so as to provide between 15 per cent and 20 per cent of M.P.s. The Commission calculated that this degree of proportionality would have produced single party majority governments in three out of the last four elections and a hung Parliament, where no party has a majority, only in 1992. The Liberal Democrat party would be the main beneficiary of the change by receiving a more proportional share of seats. The boundary changes necessitated by these recommendations made it impossible for it to come into effect at the next election regardless of when the referendum was held.

Meanwhile there are already a number of electoral systems using proportional representation in existence in the United Kingdom. The devolved Parliament in Scotland and the devolved Assembly in Wales are elected by the Additional Member System with constituency M.P.s elected by first past the post voting and additional M.P.s taken from a party list to achieve proportionality in accordance with a second vote for the party. In neither country did Labour achieve an overall majority, though it was the largest party. This led to a coalition with the Liberal Democrats (who came fourth) in Scotland but at first to a minority administration in Wales. It was precisely to avoid one party dominance in these countries that proportional representation was introduced. For similar reasons the Northern Ireland Assembly is elected by proportional representation, in this case the single transferable vote (Northern Ireland (Elections) Act 1998). The British Members of the European Parliament (M.E.P.s) are also elected by proportional representation to bring the United Kingdom into line with other European countries. In this case the system chosen was a closed regional list system, where votes are cast for a party (or an independent candidate) and seats are filled from the party lists in proportion to votes cast for the party and in the order in which candidates appear on the list (European Parliamentary Elections Act 1999). The inability to vote for a specific candidate caused so much controversy, particularly in the House of Lords, that the Act only became law by use of the Parliament Act 1949 to override the veto of the House of Lords (see below, Chapter 2).

Members of the Greater London Assembly are also chosen by the Additional Member System whilst the mayor for Greater London is chosen by the Supplementary Vote, a variant of the Alternative Vote where voters can only express two preferences. In Scotland there has been agreement in principle that local councils should be elected by a proportional electoral system, again to avoid one party dominance.

This proliferation of different proportional electoral systems shows that there is no "best buy" electoral system but that it has to be tailored to fit the type of body which is being elected, its purpose and functions and the political context in which the elections take place. The main purpose of elections for the Westminster Parliament is to choose the government.

CHOICE OF PRIME MINISTER

This brings us to the choice of Prime Minister who heads the government. In law it is the Queen who appoints the Prime Minister; in practice she must appoint the leader of the party which has won the majority of seats in the House of Commons. This forms the crucial link between the government and Parliament. If a party wins an overall majority of seats the choice of Prime Minister is clear but even under the present electoral system this did not happen in February 1974, and if proportional representation were to be adopted it would happen less frequently. Where no party obtains a clear majority there are no legal rules, only conventional rules based on past precedents, which may not give a definitive answer because the situation is not identical and the rules are flexible. This flexibility would be lost if the rules were embodied in a written constitution. Ultimately the decision lies with the Queen and her advisers, though politicians will, if at all possible, settle the problem among themselves. What is the problem?

If the Prime Minister, who remains in office during the General Election, loses his overall majority he may try, as Mr Heath did in 1974, to form a coalition with another party in order to obtain such a majority. If he fails he should resign, as Mr Heath did, whether or not his party has won more seats than any other party (as Mr Heath's did not in 1974). For the only alternative to resignation would be to ask the Queen to dissolve Parliament again and hold another election; and for this there is no precedent. The leader of the party with the next highest number of seats should, therefore, be asked to form a government. Unless he forms a coalition and obtains an overall majority he will be in a minority and risk defeat in the House of Commons. If this happens very soon, at the end of the debate on the Queen's speech, the problem arises whether he is entitled to ask the Queen to dissolve Parliament or whether she could refuse his request and ask the leader of the third party to try to form a government. In 1974 the minority Labour government was not defeated in this way and the Prime Minister did not ask for a dissolution until eight months had elapsed after the previous General Election. Whichever action the Queen took would involve her in controversy. To refuse the Prime Minister a dissolution would be unprecedented in modern times. To grant one so soon after the previous election would not only be undesirable but might lay her open to charges of partiality if she had already refused one to the outgoing Prime Minister. The only way out of this dilemma is for the parties to reach agreement among themselves either by forming a coalition or, if this is not possible, to allow a minority government a breathing space in which to govern, as happened in 1974.

A similar problem would arise if a coalition government had been formed and one of the partners left the government so that it no longer had a majority in the House of Commons. If the Prime Minister of the minority government were to ask the Queen for a dissolution of Parliament could she refuse if the party who left the government now supported the opposition who thus had a majority in the House of Commons? This happened in Germany in 1982 but, unlike Germany, we have no constitution which regulates such a situation. The convention that the Queen must act on the advice of the Prime Minister conflicts with that which obliges her to appoint as Prime Minister the person who commands a majority in the Commons. Once again, to refuse a dissolution would involve the Queen in controversy whereas to grant one would only do so if it was very soon after a General Election or it was in war-time or at a time of national emergency.

The appointment of a Prime Minister may also arise when the existing one dies or resigns from office. The Conservatives did not elect their leader until 1965, so that when Harold Macmillan resigned as Prime Minister in 1963, the Queen was at least formally involved in the controversy surrounding the choice of a successor. The three main parties have very different rules for the election of a leader. The Liberal Democrat leader is elected by all the members of the party. Since 1981 the Labour leader is elected by an electoral college consisting of Labour M.P.s (one-third), the constituency Labour parties (one-third) and the trade unions (one-third) with voting taking place on the basis of one member-one vote. This could at some future time cause constitutional problems if the leader so chosen was not acceptable to Labour M.P.s on whose loyalty a Labour Prime Minister would depend. The electorate for the Conservative leader used to consist effectively of Conservative M.P.s but the procedure was a complex one and made constitutional history when it was used in November 1990 to oust Mrs Thatcher as Prime Minister.

The uniqueness of what happened in 1990 lay in the fact that the Prime Minister lost office not as a result of an election defeat or the break up of a coalition government or being forced to resign due to ill-health or a vote in the House of Commons, nor was it a voluntary retirement. Mrs Thatcher was the first Prime Minister to be voted out of office by M.P.s of her own party. This could only happen because there was provision in the rules of the Conservative party since 1975 for an annual election whether the party was in office or not. A Labour Prime Minister can only be challenged at the Party conference if a majority on a card vote calls for an election. In 1990 it only needed a proposer and seconder whose names had to be published to nominate a rival candidate in the Conservative party. Mrs Thatcher received an overall majority but fell short by four votes of the 15 per cent of those entitled to vote by which she had to exceed her nearest rival. At the last minute she withdrew from the second ballot for which only an absolute majority of those entitled to vote was needed. Mr Major fell two votes short of an absolute majority but his nearest rival, Mr Heseltine, conceded defeat.

As a result of what happened to Mrs Thatcher the rules were changed in 1991 to require an election to be requested by 10 per cent of Conservative M.P.s before nominations could be made. Nevertheless, Mr Major felt so vulnerable to a challenge in 1995 that he precipitated an election by the unprecedented step of resigning the leadership whilst remaining as Prime Minister and then standing as a candidate in the ensuing election, which he won handsomely. In 1996 Conservative M.P.s decided to ban any challenge to Mr Major before the 1997 General Election. The overwhelming defeat of the Conservatives in that election led to fundamental changes in the rules but not until after the election of the new leader, Mr Hague.

A challenge to the leader can now be mounted only if he or she has lost a vote of confidence held at the request of at least 15 per cent of Conservative M.P.s or of the leader himself. M.P.s will then (or if there is a vacancy) hold ballots until the number of candidates is reduced to two. A postal ballot of all members of the Conservative party will finally be held to choose the winning candidate. The role of the extra-parliamentary party is, therefore, much more limited in the election of the Conservative leader than in the case of the Liberal Democrats or even the Labour party.

The constitutional significance of these leadership election rules is that they enable a Prime Minister to be dismissed without a General Election as has happened on previous occasions through resignations forced or otherwise. More importantly, in the context of whether Britain is an elective dictatorship, it shows that there are constitutional mechanisms other than a General Election for removing the alleged dictator. This is very relevant to the debate about whether we have Prime Ministerial or Cabinet government which will now be examined.

PRIME MINISTER'S POWERS

Appointment and dismissal of ministers

The first and perhaps foremost power of the Prime Minister is that of appointing and dismissing ministers. In law, appointments are made by the Queen; by convention the power is exercised on the advice of the Prime Minister. The most important constitutional constraint, which again has grown up through convention, is that ministers must be or become members of either the House of Commons or the House of Lords. The holders of the most important offices (including the Prime Ministership itself) normally sit in the Commons, though there have been some notable exceptions such as Lord Carrington (Minister of Defence and Foreign Secretary) and Lord Young (Employment Secretary). The most important officeholders and other ministers of the Prime Minister's choosing are appointed members of the Cabinet which normally has between 20 and 25 members. This is the body which Bagehot (1867, p.68) called 'a *hyphen* which joins, a *buckle* which fastens, the legislative part of the State to the executive part of the State'.

There are, of course, political constraints on the Prime Minister in appointing ministers. Senior members of the governing party, *e.g.* those who sat on the opposition front bench, will have a prior claim to be considered. But the situation would be transformed if, as Mr Benn (1980) has suggested, the Cabinet were elected by the M.P.s of the party in power in the same way as Labour MPs elect their Shadow Cabinet which, in accordance with Standing Orders of the Labour Party, has to become the Cabinet when Labour wins the election. This does not, however, bind a Labour Prime Minister and Mr. Blair, in at least one case, breached the rule. The power of the Prime Minister would be curtailed even more drastically by Mr Benn's suggestion for annual elections, for this would take away the power of dismissal, which is the most potent instrument for moulding the Cabinet to the Prime Minister's will. The limits on this power are personal and political. Some Prime Ministers are more ruthless than others. The political constraints involve balancing the risks of opposition from the ex-minister on the back benches with those from keeping him within the Cabinet. Mr Benn was never dismissed from the Labour Cabinet, while Mrs Thatcher steadily eliminated her opponents from her government. Mr Macmillan dismissed seven Cabinet ministers at one time in 1962. The political repercussions of such actions may not be immediately apparent. The penalty may not be paid until the next election in lost popularity. Before then it may lead to more opposition from the government back benches. In the case of Mrs Thatcher former Cabinet ministers played a leading part in her downfall.

Relationship between Prime Minister and Cabinet

The relationship between the Prime Minister and his Cabinet is also very much a matter of personalities, both his and theirs. The proponents of Prime Ministerial power point to the power to control the agenda of Cabinet meetings, the use of Cabinet committees appointed by the Prime Minister or informal groups of ministers or bilateral discussions between the Prime Minister and a minister instead of the full Cabinet for decision-making, the power derived from presiding over the Cabinet and summing up its discussions, and the close relationship with the Secretary to the Cabinet who is also the Head of the Civil Service. Each Prime Minister uses these powers differently and since Cabinet proceedings are held in secret we have to rely on the conflicting accounts of the participants after the event and unattributable leaks at the time. After 30 years Cabinet documents are made public (Public Records Acts 1958 and 1967, Freedom of Information Act, 2000; Part VI). Exceptionally Cabinet documents may be made available to a committee of inquiry as happened in the case of the Franks review of the Falkland Islands (Cmnd. 8787, 1983, and the Scott inquiry into Arms Exports to Iraq (H.C. 115, 1995–96). Even more exceptionally, Cabinet secrets may be openly bandied about in the press and the House of Commons as happened in the controversy over the rescue of the Westland Helicopter Company. From these sources it is becoming increasingly clear that the Cabinet is no longer the strategic decision-making body which is implied in the phrase "Cabinet government". Not only is the agenda pre-empted by routine business and one-off cases which could not be resolved elsewhere but some very important issues have not been discussed there. These include Britain's atom bomb under Attlee, the Suez intervention by Eden, devaluation of the pound by Wilson, devolving the fixing of interest rates to the Bank of England under Mr. Blair, and, under Mrs Thatcher, the Falklands issue prior to the Argentine invasion, the banning of trade unions at GCHQ, the granting of consent to the USA to use its British bases for the bombing of Libya, and the rescue of the Westland Helicopter Company. It was Mrs Thatcher's refusal to allow this last issue to be discussed in Cabinet that led Mr Heseltine, the Defence Secretary, to charge Mrs Thatcher with responsibility for "the breakdown of constitutional government" (*Observer*, January 12, 1986). The former Prime Minister, Mr Callaghan, thought this was overegging the pudding and put the blame squarely on the Cabinet. It was up to them to decide what they would put up with, "If they behave like mice they must expect to be chased" (H.C. Deb., vol. 89, col. 1115, January 15, 1986). The ultimate weapon that a member of the

Cabinet can use if he does not approve of what is being done in or outside the Cabinet is to resign, as Mr Heseltine did, but the weapon may turn out to be a boomerang.

COLLECTIVE RESPONSIBILITY

When a minister resigns because of disagreement with the Prime Minister and his colleagues he is observing the convention of collective responsibility. According to this rule of the constitution, each member of the government must support the government's decisions inside Parliament and outside. The corollary of this rule is Cabinet secrecy. The public unanimity would be exposed as a sham if the private disagreements were immediately revealed, or they would not be expressed if the participants knew in advance that they would be revealed publicly later. These considerations become weaker with the lapse of time. Though the 30-year rule marks the legal termination of secrecy, 15 years was accepted as a conventional guideline for disclosure by ministers of confidential Cabinet discussions (Cmnd 6386, 1976). This followed the unsuccessful attempt to stop the publication of the sensational Crossman *Diaries* which revealed the inner workings of Mr. Wilson's first government ten years later when Labour was again in power (*AG v. Jonathan Cape Ltd*, 1976). These revelations seem rather tame in the light of subsequent memoirs by ex-Prime Ministers and Ministers of which John Major's and Norman Lamont's autobiographies are recent examples. Both the unanimity rule and the secrecy rule have been more honoured in the breach than the observance. The rationale of the convention is to strengthen the government in whom public confidence is undermined by the exposure of open disagreements. But there have been occasions when open disagreement has been the only mechanism to prevent the government splitting apart and the convention has been deliberately set aside by an agreement to differ. This happened for the first time in 1932 in the case of a coalition government but it did not prevent the dissenting ministers resigning shortly afterwards. Mr Wilson followed this precedent in 1975, allowing open disagreement between members of the government over the government's recommendation to remain in the EEC, during the referendum campaign (H.C. Deb., vol. 889, col. 351, *Written Answers*, April 7, 1975). He did not extend this freedom to parliamentary proceedings and dismissed Mr Heffer for breaking this rule. Mr Callaghan set aside the convention in 1977 when allowing a free vote on a government Bill providing for direct elections to the European Assembly but did not extend this freedom to speaking against the Bill. When asked about this decision he made the revealing remark, "I certainly think that the doctrine should apply, except in cases where I announce that it does not" (H.C. Deb., vol. 933, col. 552, June 16, 1977). Is the unanimity and secrecy convention a rule the Prime Minister can use or not to strengthen his position? The waiver of the rule can be seen in this light but it can also be regarded as a desperate remedy to prevent the government from disintegrating.

Unattributable leaks relating to Cabinet discussions are another safety-valve to preserve the façade of unanimity while at the same time allowing the hidden disagreements to surface without the source being revealed. These leaks may come from the Prime Minister as well as from dissenting ministers. Again Mr Callaghan spoke memorably: "You know the difference between leaking and briefing. Briefing is what I do and leaking is what you do" (Cmnd. 5104, vol. 4, p. 187, 1972).

Leaking still pays lip service to the rule, open disagreement between ministers breaks it. No Prime Minister can welcome this; it is a sign of weakness, not strength. To assert his authority, the Prime Minister must try to silence the minister or dismiss him. It was Mrs Thatcher's ultimatum to Mr Heseltine to observe collective responsibility in the Westland Helicopters affair that precipitated his walk-out from the Cabinet after retorting that he would accept collective responsibility where there had been collective decision-making. This correlation has not existed since the classic days of Cabinet government described by Bagehot. The unanimity rule has long been extended beyond members of the Cabinet and, as we have seen, the Cabinet is no longer the sole decision-making body. The acceleration of this trend under Mrs Thatcher was the basic constitutional issue raised by Mr Heseltine. There was for a brief period a return to more collective decision-making under John Major but the decision to close down over 30 pits with the loss of 30,000 mining jobs was taken by key ministers in economic departments but without the approval of the Cabinet (*The Times*, October 16, 1992).

Mr Blair's style is nearer to Mrs Thatcher's and the Cabinet is moving ever closer to becoming a dignified rather than efficient part of the Constitution, as Mr Crossman asserted in 1963 in his Introduction to Bagehot (p. 54). A novel development under Mr Blair has been the setting up of a Joint Consultative Committee of the Cabinet which consists of Ministers and Liberal Democrat

M.P.s to discuss constitutional reform. It is not a decision-making body and the Liberal Democrat members are not bound by collective responsibility.

The other aspect of collective responsibility, namely responsibility to the House of Commons, is the fulcrum on which our parliamentary democracy turns. The House of Commons holds the power of life and death over the government but equally the Prime Minister can destroy Parliament by asking for a dissolution. The government can govern only so long as it does not lose the support of the House of Commons. If it does, today, in contrast to the earlier part of the nineteenth century, this would inevitably lead to a General Election. Again, in contrast to the earlier part of the nineteenth century, we have a rigid party system with strict discipline and loyalty. A government which holds a majority in the House of Commons can only be defeated as a result of a revolt by its own backbenchers, who know that a successful revolt will place their own seats in jeopardy at the ensuing General Election. It is not, therefore, surprising that the only two governments to be defeated on a vote of confidence this century have been minority governments, both Labour governments in 1924 and 1979. If the Leader of the Opposition puts down a motion of no confidence the government must by convention provide time for its early debate. The government may also itself seek a vote of confidence or deliberately make an issue one of confidence in order to put the maximum pressure on its supporters, though it is at the same time putting its life in their hands. It can also use a vote of confidence on an issue to reverse a previous defeat on the issue or alternatively it can accept the defeat. In the past a defeat on a major issue was regarded as a matter of confidence but governments no longer treat them as such. This development has enabled governments, in particular minority governments, to survive longer but it has also enabled backbenchers, especially rebel government backbenchers, to score victories against the government.

It is also possible to have a hidden vote of confidence. This happened on November 4, 1992 (H.C. Deb., vol. 213, col. 283) on the European Communities (Amendment) Bill which enacts the Maastricht Treaty into U.K. law. The Bill had been halted by the "No" vote in the Danish referendum and the government had promised a further debate before continuing with the Bill. In order to rally the maximum support from the Euro-sceptic M.P.s in the Conservative party the government privately signalled the vote as one of confidence but publicly put down an anodyne motion to proceed with the Bill. The Labour opposition treated the vote as one of confidence in the government and voted against the motion whilst the Liberal Democrats supported the motion. The government scraped home by three votes after much arm-twisting and last minute concessions to its rebel M.P.s (Baker, Gamble and Ludlam 1993, p. 151). In the end the government was forced to bring its rebels into line on the Maastricht Treaty by an explicit vote of confidence (see below Chapter 3).

The convention of collective responsibility, the linchpin of our democracy, has thus contracted considerably in scope. It is now analogous to the ultimate deterrent whose fall-out is as lethal to those who use it as to those against whom it is used. The parallel convention of the individual responsibility of ministers has also undergone fundamental change.

INDIVIDUAL RESPONSIBILITY

The responsibility of individual ministers to the House of Commons can ultimately be enforced by the same mechanism as the collective responsibility of the government, namely by a vote of no confidence or censure. Though such a vote is not strictly one of confidence in the government, such a motion put down by the opposition will make the government side close ranks, and party discipline and loyalty will make the result a foregone conclusion. Individual responsibility is, therefore, brought about by other means. One must distinguish the responsibility of a minister for a matter of policy, for his personal behaviour and for the mistakes of his Department, though these do not form watertight categories.

Individual responsibility of ministers for policy matters merges into collective responsibility, for if the government disassociates itself from the policy of one of its members it is asserting collective responsibility in the same way as when a minister resigns because of policy disagreements with his colleagues. The resignation of Sir Samuel Hoare as Foreign Secretary in 1935, when the government repudiated the Hoare-Laval pact ceding Abyssinia to Italy because of the public outcry, can be seen as an example of such a resignation. However, the government had to admit to an error of judgment in first accepting the proposals, an error for which they did not offer to resign. Hoare was thus made a scapegoat for what was in effect a collective decision. Lord Carrington's resignation after the Argentine invasion of the Falkland Islands can be characterised in a similar way, for the policy prior to that invasion was that of the government and the resignation was made deliberately to conduct the lightning away from the government. Mr Lamont's resignation as Chancellor of the Exchequer can only be explained on the same lines. The Prime Minister congratulated him on his performance and said there would be no change in policy. But unlike Lord Carrington, Mr Lamont did not resign as a matter of honour, accepting responsibility for the government as a whole. He was removed in response to pressure from inside and outside the Conservative party to expiate the policy failure of the government (H.C. Deb., vol. 226, col. 279, June 9, 1993). Individual responsibility is here acting as a substitute for collective responsibility.

There is a similar blurring between individual and collective responsibility where the personal behaviour of a minister is under attack. The resignation of such a minister depends very much on the attitude of his colleagues and particularly that of the Prime Minister, though they are of course subject to outside pressures. Where the misconduct of the minister is not very serious, the Prime Minister can refuse to accept his resignation and thus condone his conduct, as happened in the case of Mr Robert Dunn, a junior Education Minister whose entry in *Who's Who* was misleading about his academic qualifications (*Guardian*, May 9, 1986). In effect he was protected with the shield of collective responsibility. If the public is sufficiently outraged this may not be politically possible. This happened in the case of Mr Cecil Parkinson. Mrs Thatcher stood by him at first when the affair with his secretary became public after the General Election of 1983. But after her revelations to *The Times* the public outcry and pressure within the party forced Mrs Thatcher to accept his resignation. Embarrassment to the government and the party also finally led to the resignation of Mr David Mellor over his affair with an actress and accepting free holidays, after an initial stand supported by the Prime Minister against being hounded from office by newspapers using unethical methods of investigation (Doig, 1993). Mr Mates' resignation over his involvement with Mr Nadir must be added to this list (HC Deb., vol. 227 col. 823, June 29, 1993). Similarly Mr Macmillan could not have shielded Mr Profumo, who lied to the House over his affair with Christine Keeler. That a Prime Minister cannot always save a minister whose personal conduct is under attack is well illustrated by Mr Brittan's resignation over his leaking of a confidential letter from the Solicitor-General to Mr Heseltine during the Westland Helicopters affair. As Mr Brittan wrote in his resignation letter, he could no longer command the full confidence of his colleagues once he had been identified as the leaker, even though, as Mrs Thatcher wrote in her reply (in words similar to those in her reply to Lord Carrington's resignation), she had tried her utmost to dissuade him from resigning (*Guardian*, January 25, 1986). Mr Mandelson uniquely resigned from Mr Blair's cabinet twice within two years over issues of personal conduct, having been taken back into the cabinet ten months after his resignation in December 1998. These cases demonstrate the limits on Prime Ministerial power to save a minister, limits imposed by public opinion, by colleagues collectively and by the sense of honour of individual ministers.

It has been argued that similar considerations apply to the responsibility of a minister for mistakes made by his Department (Finer, 1956, p. 394). The resignation of Sir Thomas Dugdale in 1954 over mismanagement in his Department of the sale of a piece of land called Crichel Down is the classic and arguably the last illustration of a minister resigning for the faults of his civil servants of which he neither knew nor could have known. A former colleague, Lord Boyle (1980, p.10), has claimed that Dugdale resigned because he stood by his decision rather than for the misconduct of his officials. His resignation was certainly not required according to the rules laid down by the Home Secretary in the debate on the matter (H.C. Deb., vol. 530, col. 1285, July 20, 1954). The civil servants were not carrying out his orders or acting in accordance with his policy. He did not have to defend the misconduct of his officials but he had to render an account to Parliament of his stewardship. Mr Prior rejected the *Crichel Down* case as a precedent when he was under pressure to resign after the mass break-out from the Maze Prison in Northern Ireland. He argued that it was not his policy that was to blame but failures in carrying out security procedures at the prison (H.C. Deb., vol. 53, col. 1041, February 9, 1984). This distinction between policy and administration was strongly criticised by M.P.s but it is difficult not to agree with the verdict of his junior minister that the constitutional convention requiring ministerial resignation in such a case "had not existed in politics in this country for many years" (*ibid.*, col. 1108). Mr Baker took a similar line over the escape of IRA suspects from Brixton prison and refused to resign (H.C. Deb., vol. 194, col. 649, July 8, 1991), as did Mr Howard over break-outs from Parkhurst prison in 1995. Instead Mr Howard allegedly forced the Director-General of the Prison Service to dismiss the governor of Parkhurst, though this was an operational decision to be taken by the Director-General, who was later sacked himself (H.C. Deb. vol. 294, cols 398 and 461, May 19, 1997). This brings us to the constitutional position of the civil service.

CIVIL SERVICE

The convention of ministerial responsibility regulates not only the relationship between ministers and the House of Commons but conversely that between ministers and civil servants. Civil servants are not elected but appointed officials who are responsible to their ministers. They advise ministers on the formulation of policy and carry it out. As a corollary they are normally protected by anonymity and are politically neutral, serving each government in turn. This relationship has been subjected to great strains recently and its hallmarks are being challenged and eroded by both ministers and civil servants.

The bedrock of political neutrality on which our permanent civil service is anchored has been threatened from several directions. Civil servants are recruited on merit through fair and open competition by, or under the supervision of, independent Civil Service Commissioners. However, in recent years ministers and particularly the Prime Minister have been more involved in promotion to very senior posts and there have been a substantial number of appointments of outsiders to such posts. Mrs Thatcher was widely credited with asking whether the appointee was "one of us". This did not mean someone who was a Conservative but a person in tune with the style and ethos of the government. Since most Permanent Secretaries, who are the civil servants heading government departments, have been appointed since 1979, when the Conservatives came to power, this has profound significance for a subsequent government of a different party political complexion.

One of the first acts of the incoming new Labour government in 1997 was to staff the Prime Minister's Office, which immediately raised controversy over blurring the line between civil servants who must be politically neutral and special advisers (first appointed by Harold Wilson's government in 1974) who are politically committed to the party in power and change with the government. Mr Blair appointed many more special advisers to his office (about 30) than the previous government, as did other ministers (about 80 in total). Controversy centred in particular on two key posts, the Prime Minister's Press Secretary (Alastair Campbell) and his Chief-of-Staff (Jonathan Powell). Like all special advisers, they are civil servants paid out of public funds but they are not recruited after fair and open competition and they do not have to be impartial or politically neutral. A special Civil Service Order in Council had to be made for these two posts to enable the appointees to have executive authority over civil servants rather than purely advisory functions. The Head of the Civil Service blocked the appointment of Mr Powell as the Prime Minister's Principal Private Secretary, a post traditionally held by a career civil servant (*The Guardian*, June 3, 1997 and H.C. 285 (1997–98), Q55 seq, Select Committee on Public Administration).

The Prime Minister's Press Secretary has been even more at the centre of controversy. He attends both the Cabinet and Labour Party Conferences. He briefs the press as the Prime Minister's official spokesman where he has to tread a very fine line between the promotion and defence of government policy and the promotion and defence of the ruling party's policy (H.C. 770 (1997–98) para. 25, Select Committee on Public Administration). His overtly political stance led to calls by some members of the Opposition for him to be paid from party funds. Mrs Thatcher's Press Chief, Sir Bernard Ingham, who was a career civil servant, was just as partisan but did not attend Conservative party conferences.

In a big shake-up of the Government Information and Communication Service many directors of information, who are career civil servants, were replaced, some because of tensions between them and ministers or their special advisers. At the same time a powerful Strategic Communications Unit which includes two special advisers and reports to the Chief Press Secretary has been set up to co-ordinate the dissemination of government policy. This again has the potential to blur the line between the civil service and the party in power (H.C. 770 (1997–98) para. 23).

The most worrying example of this development is the appointment as Chief Economic Adviser to the Treasury of one of the Chancellor of the Exchequer's Special Advisers, Ed Balls. By this means one of the most senior posts in the Treasury has been filled by a political appointment which does not have to follow the procedures for the appointment of civil servants (*The Guardian*, October 23, 1999). These procedures were observed for one of his predecessors, Sir Terry Burns, an academic recruited by the Conservatives, who had become Permanent Secretary at the Treasury when Labour took office in 1997. He took early retirement a year later because of disagreements with the Chancellor and his special advisers (*The Guardian*, June 3, 1998). The politici-sation of the civil service is thus being accelerated under the Labour government rather than reversed.

At the same time that the government is increasing its political influence over the civil service it is reasserting its duty to uphold the political impartiality of civil servants and not to ask them to engage in activities which would call this into question (Ministerial Code of Conduct, Cabinet Office, 1997, para. 56). An almost identical formulation of ministerial duties *vis-à-vis* the civil service did not prevent a previous government from misus-ing civil servants for party political purposes. The most notorious example was the use of a civil servant to leak the Solicitor-General's letter in the Westland affair and Mrs Thatcher said she deeply regretted the method used for bringing the letter into the public domain (H.C. Deb., vol. 90, col. 653, January 27, 1986).

The position of civil servants who are asked to perform actions which they consider unethical was addressed in the revised note of guidance from the Head of the Civil Service on the duties and responsibilities of civil servants (H.C. Deb., vol. 123, col. 572, *Written Answers*, December 2, 1987). The original guidelines were drawn up following the *Ponting* case. Mr Ponting, a civil servant in the Ministry of Defence, leaked information to an M.P. because he felt that ministers were withholding information from a com-mittee of the House of Commons. He was later acquitted for leak-ing confidential information contrary to the Official Secrets Act 1911. In such cases the guidelines provided for the matter to be reported to a senior officer and if appropriate to the Permanent Head of the Department. Whether this provision would have helped Mr Ponting is doubtful, it certainly did not help the civil servant who was asked to leak the Solicitor-General's letter in the Westland affair as her Head of Department was not available (H.C. 519, (1985–86) para. 174). In the last resort there was an appeal to the Head of the Civil Service. This was only used once (H.C. 27 (1993–94) para. 97, Treasury and Civil Service Committee).

On January 1, 1996 there came into operation a Civil Service Code which now codifies the constitutional role and responsibil-ities of civil servants both *vis-à-vis* ministers and the public. It re-affirms the duty of ministers to uphold the political impartiality of the civil service and not to ask civil servants to act in any way which would conflict with the Civil Service Code. More specifi-cally it provides that where a civil servant is being asked to act illegally, improperly, unethically or in breach of constitutional convention he may report the matter to his department or agency and, if not satisfied with the response, report it to the Civil Service Commissioners. So there is for the first time an independent body to which civil servants can appeal when asked to act improperly by ministers.

The Civil Service Code enshrines the model of how ministers and civil servants should behave; the Scott Report into the Export of Arms to Iraq (H.C. 115 (1995–96) and its aftermath document the pathology of their behaviour. A number of civil servants were severely criticised in the report for drafting misleading answers to Parliamentary questions and for misleading the courts. In all but two cases it was concluded that disciplinary action was not appropriate "because the officials concerned had acted in good faith, conscientiously and in accordance with government policy" (H.C. 285 (1997–98), Appendix 2). To put it more crudely, as no minister resigned it would have been unfair to punish the civil servants involved. Foreign Office officials, whose interference with the course of justice led to the quashing of criminal convictions for illegal arms exports (the *Dunk* case), were not prosecuted due to the refusal of witnesses to give evidence. However, the Foreign Office paid out £125,000 in compensation arising from the conduct of two officials (*The Guardian*, October 31, 2000) but their conduct did not prevent them becoming respectively a High Commissioner and a Deputy High Commissioner. It was later reported to a House of Commons committee that two Foreign Office officials have been subject to disciplinary action (H.C. 285, 1997–98, Appendix 2). In accordance with Government guidelines, the identity of such individuals is kept confidential (*ibid.*), whereas the Scott Report freely identified the civil servants by name. This inquiry provides another illustration of the shield of anonymity being removed from civil servants. This also happened following the inquiry into the leak of the Solicitor-General's letter in the Westland affair, though in that case the civil servants were not allowed to defend themselves before the House of Commons committee investigating the issue because the Government insisted, in strict compliance with the convention of ministerial responsibility, that it is for ministers to investigate the conduct of civil servants and to decide which officials appear before these committees (H.C. 169, 1985–86, Q 1064, Evidence to the Defence Committee). The government's position has not changed in this respect and ministers will only reveal details of disciplinary action against civil servants to committees in confidence (H.C. 285 (1997–98), Appendix 2).

However, civil servants are increasingly giving evidence in public to parliamentary committees about departmental policies and their implementation. This brings officials into the public eye and identifies them more openly with government policies. But they still appear on behalf of ministers to whom they are accountable for what they say and thus the figleaf of ministerial responsibility remains intact.

It has slipped badly as a result of developments which are moving in the direction of privatisation of the civil service. Over three-quarters of the civil service has been reorganised into executive agencies which deliver public services, such as the Social Security Benefits Agency for the payment of social security benefits, the Driver and Vehicle licensing agency, the Meteorological Office, the Passport Office and up to 140 others. It is envisaged that only a small core of the civil service will eventually remain in conventional government departments. These agencies operate within the guidance laid down by framework documents which govern the policy and financial targets to be followed. This reorganisation has had important repercussions for accountability. Though lip-service is paid to ministerial responsibility, it is the Chief Executive of the agency, who is increasingly likely to be recruited from outside the civil service, who is held to account before committees of the House of Commons and who cannot hide behind the minister in respect of matters within his delegated responsibility. Again, though parliamentary questions can still be addressed to ministers, those concerned with operational rather than policy matters are referred to the Chief Executive who writes to the M.P. After much pressure from M.P.s these letters are now published in Hansard.

With the creation of executive agencies accountability has acquired a new meaning. Agencies are set performance as well as financial targets. They will be assessed by how far they achieve these targets and the pay of their Chief Executive can be affected accordingly. It is a business ethos rather than a public service culture which will predominate. The prevailing values will be economic and measurable rather than non-material and unquantifiable, *i.e.* efficiency as against fairness. The Citizen's Charter (now Service First) which applies to the public services reinforces this trend by stressing performance indicators, complaints machinery and compensation for failing to meet targets. It sees the citizen as a customer of public services not as a member of a community whose needs have to be evaluated against those of others.

The same ethos is being further promoted by the contracting-out of services to the private sector. The running of certain prisons and the escort of prisoners by a private company, Group 4, are the fruits of this development. Ultimately there may be full privatisation such as the sale of the Property Services Agency and Her Majesty's Stationery Office.

Privatisation and politicisation are the Scylla and Charybdis threatening the civil service. The Labour government which took office in 1997 far from reversing has accelerated these developments. It has increased the influence and numbers of political advisers and it is intensifying the business ethos through public service agreements setting measurable targets for the government's objectives in each department (Public Service Agreements, Cm 4181, 1999). There has been a marked increase in the centralisation of power through the Prime Minister's office and the modernisation of the civil service will emphasise the entrepreneurial ethos rather than the public service values of impartiality, objectivity and integrity (Modernising Government, Cm 4310, 1999). It is not coincidental that these developments are imports from the USA where the higher echelons of the civil service change with the President. This takes place, however, in the context of a written constitution based on the separation of the executive, legislative and judicial powers so that each can be a check on the other, in contrast to the sovereignty of Parliament which we must now examine in operation.

2

PARLIAMENT

THE HOUSE OF COMMONS

The House of Commons, which is the elected Chamber (the House of Lords will be discussed later), has a dual function: its role is both to sustain the government and to criticise it. This dichotomy runs through much of the work of the House of Commons and is the key to understanding the paradox that often Parliament is used as a synonym for the government because it acts as a rubber stamp; but it is also used in antithesis to the government, *i.e.* as a control mechanism. It would not be a solution to this conflict to say that the majority of the House fulfil one function and the opposition another, for the role of critic is performed by both sides of the House. Nor would it be correct to say that the role varies according to which task the House is performing, *i.e.* whether it is legislating or asking questions, for its critical and sustaining roles cut across these functions. It is when voting rather than expressing opinions that this dual role becomes most sharply focused, for M.P.s then have to make a clear decision as to whether to support the government or not. A vote of no confidence is, as we have seen, the ultimate weapon for defeating a government but almost certainly today at the cost of a dissolution of Parliament. Defeats on other issues illustrate the controlling function better because, unlike the bee's sting, they can be used more than once. Even these are likely to be rare and it is the daily give and take of debate and questioning which bring pressure to bear on the government, particularly under the constraints of time and coupled with the threat of possible defeat, that wring concessions and compromises from the government, thus still making the House of Commons (and to a lesser extent the House of Lords) an important check on the elective dictatorship of the government.

That this check is by no means as powerful as it was in the nineteenth century is due to the growth of the party system which controls, first, who gets elected as an M.P. and then how he votes once he is an M.P. We have seen how difficult it is under our electoral system to be elected unless one belongs to one of the two main parties; it is virtually impossible if one belongs to no party, though there have been some isolated exceptions. Once elected, the M.P. is the representative of his constituency which, as Edmund Burke made clear in his famous address to his Bristol constituents in 1774, does not constrain him to vote in accordance with their interests, *i.e.* he is not their delegate. In fact it is a breach of privilege of the House punishable as contempt for an M.P.'s freedom of action to be fettered by an outside body. This has given rise to problems where M.P.s are sponsored by a trade union who contribute to his expenses or where they have other outside paid interests such as directorships or consultancies. Such interests are not banned, because the House would then become a body of professional politicians, but the House has resolved that they must be disclosed in debate and other proceedings and declared in a register of interests open to public inspection (H.C. Deb., vol. 874, col. 391, May 22, 1974 and vol. 227, col. 757 seq., June 28, 1993). These rules have been much strengthened as a result of the recommendations of the Committee on Standards in Public Life (First Report, Cm 2580 (1995)) which was set up following the "cash for questions" scandal involving some M.P.s who allegedly accepted payments for asking parliamentary questions. This led to the introduction of a Code of Conduct for M.P.s and a Parliamentary Commissioner for Standards, who investigates complaints against M.P.s and reports to the Committee on Standards and Privileges of the House of Commons. This committee then recommends to the House of Commons what penalty (if any) should be imposed on the M.P. The House can order the M.P. to apologise or suspend the M.P. with loss of salary for that period or in extreme cases expel the M.P. These measures are designed to prevent conflict between an M.P.s private interests and his duty to represent the public interest. In reality, however, the biggest constraint on an M.P.s freedom of action comes from the party system.

Whipping

The mechanism for exerting pressure on an M.P. to toe the party line is the system of whipping. The Chief Whip and his assistant whips are members of the government whose task it is to ensure that M.P.s on the government side vote in accordance with the party whip which is a summons to vote graded according to importance, the three-line whip being the most peremptory. The opposition operates a similar system for its members. Withdrawal of the whip is the ultimate sanction for failure to vote with the party and may be the prelude to deselection of the M.P. by his constituency party. There are many lesser pressures which can be brought to bear, varying from not being allowed to go on a trip abroad with a parliamentary delegation, to not being considered for a ministerial post and being reported to the Constituency Chairman. "One of the most brutal and controversial whipping operations for years" took place before the vote on the "paving motion" for the Maastricht Bill (Baker, Gamble and Ludlam 1993, p. 158, *supra* Chapter 1). These pressure points epitomize the bondage of an M.P. to his party which reinforces the party loyalty which an M.P. naturally feels. They also distinguish today's M.P.s from their nineteenth-century forebears, who were not dependent on their seats for their livelihood, as many M.P.s are today.

Nevertheless, the pressure does not always work and some M.P.s are known as regular rebels. The crunch comes when the rebellion is large enough to inflict defeat on the government. The increase in such defeats in the 1970s (65 defeats on the floor of the House of Commons between 1972 and 1979) has been noted (Norton, 1982, p. 112). Most of these were, however, inflicted on the minority Labour government between 1974 and 1979 and are therefore not typical for a majority government but more a foretaste of things to come under a hung Parliament. Mr. Major's government elected in 1992 with a majority of 21 was considerably hamstrung by its small majority particularly on the Maastricht Bill because of the sizeable group of rebel Euro-sceptics. Not only was the government defeated on a specific amendment on March 8, 1993 (H.C. Deb., vol. 220, col. 715), which prolonged proceedings on the Bill by the need for a further stage of debate (the report stage) but the government also had to accept crucial amendments on the U.K.'s opt-out from the social chapter of the Treaty to avoid defeat (H.C. Deb., vol. 223, col. 529, April 22, 1993 and *ibid.* vol. 224, col. 207, May 5, 1993). Also it could not use the usual mechanism for curtailing debate on a Bill, the guillotine (see below), because of the rebels on its backbenches and it had to rely on the opposition parties to move the closure when debating individual amendments. In the main votes on the principles of the Bill (the second and third readings) the government was not in danger because the Labour opposition abstained. The government was also forced into making other concessions such as the reviewing of its pit-closure programme because of rebellion in its own ranks (H.C. Deb., vol. 212, col. 205, October 19, 1992).

However, a large majority can also be dangerous for a government, as Mr Pym remarked during the 1983 General Election, a warning which probably contributed to the loss of his Cabinet post. Mrs Thatcher's government, with a majority of 146, suffered defeats, most notably on the Shops Bill providing for Sunday opening (H.C. Deb., vol. 95, col. 694, April 14, 1986). The government tried to forestall defeat by offering a free vote on the later stages of the Bill. A free vote is traditionally used for non-party political issues of conscience (*e.g.* the abolition of capital punishment) but it can also be used to prevent defeat, as happened in the case of the Bill providing for direct elections to the European Assembly. In that case the free vote extended, as we saw, to members of the government (Chapter 1). Some free votes are less free than others. In the debate on the Water (Fluoridation) Bill members of the government were whipped (*ibid.*, col. 689), and this also happened in the important debate on the procedure for Bills which will be considered shortly. Normally whipping applies not only on the floor of the House but when a Bill is considered in detail in committee. Defeats on amendments to the Bill are more frequent here because the majority of the government is smaller in proportion to the size of the committee. Such defeats can be reversed when the Bill returns to the floor of the House to be further amended. However, in the case of the Civil Aviation Bill in 1985 government rebels, who objected to the expansion of Stansted Airport, managed to get the committee stage halted altogether (Standing Committee F, February 12 1985) and the Bill was abandoned, but this did not ultimately prevent the limited expansion of Stansted Airport.

It is arguable, therefore, that M.P.s hold the control of an elective dictatorship in their own hands. They have the vote and if they used it more frequently in accordance with their judgment rather than the party whip, the power of the government would be markedly curtailed. Undoubtedly M.P.s could exercise more independence and such a development would be accelerated in a hung Parliament, *i.e.* where no party had an overall majority. But it would be simplistic to underestimate the pressures of party loyalty and the party whips. The most potent antidote to the latter would be a system of voting in secret in the House of Commons instead of by walking through the lobbies. The potency of this system was shown in Israel, for the election of the President by M.P.s, when a Labour President was elected by a majority of M.P.s of the other parties in 1983. However valid in principle the arguments in favour of secret voting may be — and it has been made obligatory for officers of trade unions (Trade Union Act 1984) — it is utopian to imagine that any government would concede the power this would confer on its backbenchers to defeat its policies with impunity except on a vote of confidence, where there would be the threat of dissolution. Such votes of confidence would probably then become more frequent.

The role of the opposition

Since such a utopian solution to the elective dictatorship is unlikely, the main burden of opposition to the government inevitably lies with the opposition. This has been institutionalised in a number of ways. Most significantly perhaps, the Leader of the Opposition is paid a salary as are a few other opposition officeholders (Ministerial and Other Salaries Act 1975 and 1997) and in addition money is made available from public funds to opposition parties for their parliamentary work (H.C. Deb., vol. 888, col. 1869, March 20, 1975 and vol. 332, col. 427, May 26, 1999). Many would like to go further in strengthening advice for the opposition, to the extent of seconding civil servants to their staff (Wass, 1983). The rights of the opposition are enshrined in the procedure of the House of Commons. As we have seen, a motion of no confidence tabled by the opposition must be debated as soon as possible. At Prime Minister's question time the Leader of the Opposition is given priority over other M.P.s. In debate speakers alternate between government and opposition, and membership of committees is proportionate to the membership of the House. One of the problems encountered by the Liberal Democrats is that House of Commons procedure is adapted for the two-party system and does not easily accommodate a third party. This has led to a series of protests to procure recognition, most notably to obtain a share of those days expressly set aside for the opposition on which they may choose the subject for debate. They are now entitled to three out of the 20 "opposition days" (see below).

Supply procedure

These "opposition days" have an interesting history which is symptomatic of the relationship between the government and the House of Commons. Their origin lies in the days set aside for the discussion of public expenditure in the form of the annual estimates which, when embodied in the annual Appropriation Acts, legalise central government expenditure for that year. Originally there was no limit on the number of days set aside for discussion of the estimates. It was Balfour in 1896 who bargained a fixed number of days in return for a fixed date by which all the estimates had to be put to the vote. On these Supply days, as they came to be called, the opposition was given the right to choose the subject for debate. Increasingly, these days have been used by the opposition to discuss government policy rather than the details of government expenditure. There was rarely even a vote taken on whether an estimate should be granted to the government, and the Appropriation Acts, which legalised the expenditure, were passed purely formally without discussion except for the occasional protest at the farce that parliamentary control of expenditure had become. In 1982 the pretence of discussing expenditure on Supply days was dropped and they became called Opposition days. In addition three days were set aside for the discussion of expenditure, to be called Estimate days (H.C. Deb., vol. 28, col. 118, July 19, 1982). These days have been used for the discussion of reports of committees of the House which have been critical of particular areas of government expenditure. The debate takes place on a motion to approve a particular estimate which is then formally passed at the end of the day. Very rarely has an amendment to reduce an estimate been put to the vote — the last time was in 1992. The House of Commons has thus abdicated its function of discussing the details of government expenditure or even challenging them to a vote, preferring instead to use the allotted time to discuss issues of government policy selected by the opposition or one of its committees. This is partly the result of the intractability of the subject-matter and the inclination of politicians to discuss politics rather than economy of expenditure, but it also shows the dangers of a time-limit by which the House has to give its approval to government business, as it deprives the opposition of its strongest weapon which is time.

Legislative procedure

This has been the main topic of debate in relation to the procedure for approving legislation other than that authorising government expenditure. The House has not abdicated its function to scrutinise the details of legislation including the annual Finance. Act which authorises taxation. Detailed discussion normally takes place not in the House as a whole, except in the case of Bills of constitutional importance such as the Maastricht Bill, but in standing committees, where the Bill is discussed clause by clause and line by line. It is here that concessions can be wrung from the government by applying pressure both from outside the House and within. A good illustration is the Police and Criminal Evidence Bill on which there were 105 sittings in committee (it had to be reintroduced after the General Election of 1983) and which ended as a very different Bill from the original one. Pressures were exerted by bodies like the Law Society, the BMA, the police and other professions outside the House, whilst the opposition and government backbenchers kept up a steady stream of amendments in the House. In many cases these were then adopted by the government in a modified form. The pressure is most potent when government backbenchers join forces with the opposition to make defeat possible. Even where this does not happen, the opposition have the weapon of time, because the government needs to get its legislative programme passed at the latest by the end of the parliamentary session (normally October/November) as it lapses otherwise unless a special motion is passed. The government has a counter-weapon, the guillotine, a procedure which fixes a timetable for a Bill and automatically cuts off debate at the stated time. This is the equivalent procedure for Bills which applies automatically in the case of the estimates.

The use of the guillotine or timetabling of Bills goes to the heart of our democratic process, *i.e.* the relationship between government and Parliament, which for this purpose means the House of Commons. It is not coincidental that since 1979 when the Conservative government came to power there have been more guillotine motions than by all the previous governments this century. Whereas between 1945 and 1951 the Labour government passed its radical programme of nationalisation and the creation of the welfare state through Parliament with the use of only three guillotines, the Conservative government of Mrs Thatcher used them for 34 Bills, nearly three times the number employed by the Labour government between 1974 and 1979 which did not have a majority most of the time. The pace did not slacken under the Labour Government elected in May 1997, who had guillotined over 20 Bills in the first three sessions (H.C. Deb., vol. 357, col. 694, November 27, 2000). This tells us much not only about the government but also about the opposition. It is indicative of the increasingly adversarial nature of party politics and the breakdown of consensus between the parties about the conduct of parliamentary business.

Not only has the number of guillotines increased in recent years but they have been imposed earlier. Guillotines used to be regarded as weapons of last resort to be imposed only after the opposition had filibustered to delay the Bill becoming law. They have been used increasingly to structure debate in committee so that discussion is not prolonged on the initial clauses and curtailed on the later ones after the guillotine has fallen (Ganz 1990, p. 496). This marked the beginning of a trend towards the automatic time-tabling of all controversial Bills which has been accelerated since 1997 by the passing for about 20 Bills of programme motions agreed between the main parties which, unlike guillotine motions, lay down an agreed time-table for discussion of the Bill and which may provide for a Business Committee to work out a detailed time-table at the committee stage of the Bill. This procedure follows the recommendations of the Modernisation Committee of the House of Commons (H.C. 190 (1997–98)) but there is still a strong division of opinion on the issue of the automatic time-tabling of Bills which cuts across party lines. The lack of consensus was clearly demonstrated in the later report of the Modernisation Committee (H.C. 589 (1999–2000) which recommended that programme motions should be applied to all Bills. Unlike previous reports it was not unanimous, with the Conservative members writing a scathing minority report in which they castigated the government for its "over-ambitious and badly drafted legislative programme" and lamented that Parliament had been marginalised and by-passed in recent years. This did not, however, prevent the proposals being approved by the House as an experiment for one session (H.C. Deb., vol. 356, col. 209 *et seq.*, November 7, 2000).

This is in marked contrast to what happened when the original recommendations of the Procedure Committee in 1985 for automatic time-tabling of Bills were debated and put to the vote. Backbenchers but not members of the government were allowed a free vote and there arose the unusual spectacle of the government uniting with the opposition to defeat its own backbenchers in order to preserve the rights of the opposition (H.C. Deb., vol. 92, col. 1083 *et seq.*, February 27, 1986). In his speech the then Leader of the House, Mr Biffen, made what is still the most powerful defence of the status quo: "All governments are tomorrow's possible opposition, and I think that my Right Hon. and Hon. Friends in their moments of supreme confidence, should consider, at least theoretically, how these proposals would bear upon the opposition. The Westminster political process is oblique and wide-ranging. It is like a seamless robe, which includes government legislation, and much else. At present, the opposition have opportunities for time and debate on legislation. If these are automatically extinguished, the opposition will be deprived of a pressure point which is often used to secure accommodation from the government, not merely on legislation, but on other points in the political process" (*ibid.*, col. 1088). The Opposition Leader of the House, Mr Shore, congratulated Mr Biffen on his far-sighted and generous speech. Unfortunately here, as elsewhere in the constitution, it may no longer be possible to rely on self-restraint by the government and constitutional changes may be necessary to hold the government in check. The Labour government elected in 1997 has made fundamental changes in the Constitution which will be considered in the following pages but these have not redressed the balance of power between the Executive and Parliament. There have been important reforms of legislative procedure such as the publication of some Bills in draft form which can then be scrutinised by a parliamentary committee and as a result may be amended by the government before starting their passage through Parliament. Other reforms to parliamentary procedure include the setting up of a parallel debating chamber in Westminster Hall, where issues can be debated without a vote being taken, enabling more backbenchers to initiate debates and more committee reports to be debated. These changes improve the mechanisms for holding the government to account but they do not alter the balance of power between Parliament and the Executive. An attempt to shift the balance by strengthening the Departmental Select Committees (H.C. 300 (1999–2000)) was promptly rejected by the government (Cm 4737). These committees must now be considered.

Select committees

The model of parliamentary government which is implicit in the extract from Mr Biffen's speech is one of adversarial politics, where the government proposes and the opposition opposes and obtains modifications of the government's proposals by internal and external pressures. There is a totally different political model, namely the consensus model, where the aim is to reach agreement across the political divide by compromise and bargaining. The end result may be similar, as compromise may be achieved by either means, but the method used will be completely different. Whether our adversarial politics is the result of our two-party system or not, the parliamentary procedures and the physical shape of the chamber of the House of Commons are geared to this system. Countries with multi-party politics have horseshoe-shaped chambers which symbolise the gradation of the political spectrum rather than its sharp division. If and when the two-party system breaks down in Britain and if proportional representation is adopted, coalition governments will have to be formed, which will involve moving towards the consensus model of politics. Even under our present adversarial system the alternative consensus model is followed in one area of House of Commons procedure, namely that of select committees. These committees, unlike the standing committees which consider legislation, do not debate but take evidence from witnesses by questions and answers and then normally make a report based on that evidence to the House as a whole. They have no powers except to make recommendations. They are constructed on the consensus model which is epitomised in their horseshoe-shaped seating arrangements.

The oldest select committee is the Public Accounts Committee which is the only mechanism by which the House of Commons examines the economy, efficiency and effectiveness of government expenditure. It has the assistance of expert auditors under the Comptroller and Auditor General whose reports to the committee form the basis of their examination of witnesses from government departments. Its chairman is by convention a senior opposition M.P., to signify its impartiality and non-partisan nature. The same applies to the committee which scrutinises delegated legislation (orders made by ministers under the authority of an Act of Parliament). The most important development of select committees came in 1979 when 14 committees (there are now 18 and some of them now cut across departmental boundaries) were set up to scrutinise the work of each government department by examining its expenditure, administration and policy. The then Leader of the House said that they could constitute the most important parliamentary reform of the century (H.C. Deb., vol. 969, col. 35, June 25, 1979) which could alter the balance of power between the government and Parliament. Has this happened?

To emphasise the independence of the new committees the nomination of their members was entrusted not to the party whips but to another committee of the House (the Committee of Selection) who have evolved their own conventions, such as the exclusion of all frontbench spokesmen, which is intended to lessen partisanship. This does not, however, mean that the whips play no role in the appointment process. It is now openly stated that the whips are the channel through which names are put forward to the Committee of Selection on behalf of the two main parties but that the Committee makes the final selection (H.C. 19, 1989–90, para. 178). However, the interference of the whips was blatantly exposed after the 1992 election when a new rule was invented by the Committee of Selection banning government backbenchers who had served for three Parliaments on a select committee. This rule was designed to bar a particular backbencher (Nicholas Winterton) from the Health Committee where he had been a thorn in the flesh of the government. It was condemned on both sides of the House which did not prevent the endorsement of the Committee's selection of M.P.s being carried by comfortable majorities (H.C. Deb., vol. 211, col. 913 *et seq.*, July 13, 1992). This highlights the innate weakness of the Departmental Committees *vis-à-vis* the government which undermines every aspect of their work.

The Committees employ expert advisers, mostly on a part-time basis and paid at a daily rate. In the session 1999–2000 there were about 100 permanent staff serving the committees (H.C. 300 (1999–2000)). They also have power to order the attendance of witnesses and the production of documents. The limits of this power can be seen in the Westland Helicopter inquiry. As we have seen, the government refused to allow the civil servants involved in the leaking of the Solicitor-General's letter to give evidence to the Defence Committee inquiring into the affair. The Committee could have enforced attendance only through an order of the House of Commons where the government had a majority. It contented itself with reporting the matter to the House in its report on the Westland affair (H.C. 519, 1985–86, para. 231). In a debate on the report the government had a majority of 157 (H.C. Deb., vol. 103, col. 416, October 29, 1986).

The withholding of evidence from the Defence Committee inquiring into the Westland affair pales into insignificance beside what happened in relation to the inquiry of the Trade & Industry Committee into the export to Iraq of a supergun. The Committee's inquiry was obstructed by its inability to obtain evidence from the Customs and Excise department and from a Conservative M.P., Sir Hal Miller (H.C. 86, 1991–92, para. 121 *et seq.*). This is in sharp contrast to the powers of the court trying three company executives of Matrix Churchill Ltd prosecuted for supplying arms-making equipment to Iraq, which ordered documents to be disclosed, including ones relating to the security services, leading to the dropping of the prosecution. Also the Committee could not have obtained from civil servants the evidence which they gave to the Scott inquiry about confidential advice to Ministers because this is ruled out by the Memorandum of Guidance for Officials appearing before Select Committees (Cabinet Office, 1997).

The latest cause célèbre concerned the investigation of arms exports to Sierra Leone by the Foreign Affairs Committee who wanted to see certain Foreign Office telegrams. Twice the Committee were denied access and made special reports in which they sought the views of the House (H.C. 760 (1997–98) and H.C. 852 (1997–98)). It was not until the Opposition made available one of their Opposition Days for a debate on the issue (H.C. Deb., vol. 315, col. 865 *et seq*, July 7, 1998) that a compromise was reached whereby summaries of the documents would be made available to the Committee together with arrangements for verifying their accuracy. After publication of the report of the inquiry into the affair set up by the Foreign Secretary, the full documents were made available. The Committee established the important constitutional principle that their investigation should not be stayed pending an inquiry by another body. But the affair also showed the weakness of their formal powers. They can only report to the House of Commons who alone can order production of the documents. As the Committee pointed out, for the House to agree such a motion "would be tantamount to a vote of no confidence in the Government" (H.C. 116 (1998–99) para. 98). In other words the vote would be a foregone conclusion. As Mr Tam Dalyell M.P. said on another occasion, "Party comes before Parliament in the House of Commons" (H.C. Deb., vol. 210, col. 810, June 30, 1992).

These high profile inquiries also illustrate one of the novel features of these committees. They can and do investigate instantaneously matters of current concern in a way that the House of Commons cannot do, namely by calling all those concerned, including ministers, to be questioned in depth and then reporting their findings to the House. The Education Committee was even able to settle an industrial dispute threatening the Proms by giving both sides an opportunity to state their case (H.C. 722, 1979–80). This function of the committees to gather information from interested parties and the government and make it available to the House and the public has received most publicity, particularly when the hearing is transmitted live on TV as was the case when the Chancellor of the Exchequer, Mr Lamont, was being questioned on the events of "Black Wednesday" when the U.K. left the ERM (H.C. 201, 1992–93, p. 1 *et seq*). The committees have contributed much to the cause of open government.

This function, however, does not fundamentally change the balance of power between government and Parliament. To do this committees must carry weight with the government and Parliament. It is very difficult to evaluate the committees' impact on the government, as they are one among many influences brought to bear. Their recommendations are most likely to bear fruit where the government is already thinking along the same lines, *e.g.* the Home Affairs Committee's report on the law relating to public order (H.C. 756, 1979–80). But they can also give an added impetus to reforms, such as the same committee's report recommending abolition of the "Sus" law, which probably would not have happened without the strong pressure of the committee (H.C. 744, 1979–80). If the committees can report before the government has crystallised its policy, they are more likely to have an impact on government policy than by criticising it *ex post facto*, though the policy-making process is a continuing one and the mere existence of the committees will make the government sensitive to their anticipated reaction, knowing that they will be called there to answer for their actions.

The impact of a committee's report is greater when it is unanimous than if it splits along party lines but this did not apply to the unanimous report of the Trade and Industry Committee on pit closures (H.C. 237, 1992–93) which was only partially accepted by the government in its White Paper "The Prospects for Coal" (Cm 2235). There have been spectacular examples of such splits, notably the Foreign Affairs Committee's report on the events surrounding the sinking of the Argentine cruiser *Belgrano* (H.C. 11, 1984–85). However, the vast majority of reports have been unanimous and where there have been votes on parts of the report these have often cut across party lines. The striving for consensus could be said to be the hallmark of the committees. It is achieved partly by the choice of subjects for investigation. It was almost inevitable that an issue as emotive as the sinking of the *Belgrano* would give rise to fundamental disagreement. This has not, however, prevented the committees from dealing with highly controversial party political issues, such as the banning of trade unions at GCHQ, and reaching consensus on them (H.C. 238, 1983–84). In other cases a party split has been avoided by not making recommendations or by openly registering disagreement in the report. But in many cases subjects would not be chosen for investigation where a party split is a foregone conclusion. The achieving of consensus is made more difficult if the draft report by the chairman is prematurely leaked so that pressures can be brought to bear on members of the committee to toe the party line rather than make the compromises necessary to reach agreement, which is more likely to be reached behind closed doors. The decision of the House to treat such leaks seriously as breaches of parliamentary privilege, and to punish them accordingly, failed at the first attempt to apply it to a *Times* journalist who published a leaked report from the Environment Committee, because the person who leaked the report to him could not be found (H.C. Deb., vol. 98, col. 293, May 20, 1986). In an exceptional case involving the Health Committee the author of a leak of the chairman's draft report to the Department of Health was discovered to be a researcher employed by a Conservative M.P. on the committee, who had tabled a series of amendments to water down criticism of the government in the report (H.C. 614, 1990–91). The M.Ps resignation was welcomed by the committee (H.C. 34, 1991–92). More recently a Labour M.P. on the Foreign Affairs Committee who leaked the draft report on arms exports to Sierra Leone (*supra*) to the Foreign Secretary resigned from the Committee and was suspended from the House for 10 days for contempt of the House (H.C. Deb. vol. 335, col. 26 *et seq*, July 12, 1999). This was the most blatant of a number of leaks since 1997 by members of committees to Ministers which seriously undermines the select committee system.

The consensus model which select committees follow is a source of weakness as well as strength. They exist as an oasis in an adversarial system. This system limits both their functions and effectiveness. If they were given powers other than the power to make recommendations, the party whips would bring to bear the same pressures on members as they do in the House itself and the committees would split along party lines. The most fundamental weakness is the difficulty in transferring the consensus of the committee to the House itself. One of the novel features of the new committees is the extent to which they have tried to dovetail their reports with the work of the House. More reports are now debated as a result of the sittings in Westminster Hall but many more are "tagged" *i.e.* mentioned as being relevant to a debate. The Estimate days are, as we have seen, used for debates on reports of the committees, though this still falls far short of a systematic examination of expenditure by the committees before approval by the House. Some of the Bills published in draft form have been considered by departmental committees and some of these committees have also made reports whilst a Bill is passing through Parliament in order to influence the legislative process. It is when such issues on which the committees have reported come to a vote in the House that the loyalty of members of the committees is put to the test. With some notable exceptions, e.g. in the debate on the "Sus" report (H.C. Deb., vol. 985, col. 1763, June 5, 1980), members have voted with their party rather than their select committee and the consensus of the committee has not been transferred to the House itself.

The most blatant example of this occurred when M.Ps on the Trade and Industry Committee openly disagreed with each other about the interpretation of their unanimous report on pit closures when the issue was debated on the floor of the House. The government obtained approval for its policy by a comfortable majority, having placated by its modifications most of the rebels who had forced it into having a review of the closure programme (H.C. Deb., vol. 222, col. 25, March 29, 1993). The same thing happened in the case of railway privatisation. The Transport Committee, chaired by a Conservative M.P. opposed to privatisation, made an interim report in time for the Bill's second reading (H.C. 375, 1992–93) and a detailed final report containing dozens of recommendations in time for the Bill's report stage on the floor of the House (H.C. 246, 1992–93). The much heralded rebellion of Conservative M.P.s collapsed when the Transport Secretary made the minimum concessions needed to buy off the rebels, in particular over the continuation of concessionary railcards after privatisation (H.C. Deb. vol. 225, col. 758 *et seq.*, May 25, 1993). More recently, a vote against the proposal for the part-privatisation of National Air Traffic Services was supported by most M.P.s on the departmental committee, which had recommended rejection of the plan, but in spite of a major rebellion by Labour backbenchers the government still had a majority of 60 (H.C. Deb. vol. 349, col. 719, *et seq*, May 9, 2000). These examples illustrate the iron law of British politics that the only way in which concessions can be wrung from a government are by a threatened rebellion in its own ranks when it has a small majority.

This cannot be altered by a reform of Departmental Select Committees on the lines suggested by the report of the Liaison Committee (which consists of all chairmen of select committees), even if these had been accepted by the government (*supra*). To free the selection of members of committees from the power of the Whips they recommended that their selection should be in the hands of three senior M.P.s acting in a non-partisan way. They wanted to make service on these committees an alternative career path for M.P.s and to counter-balance the attractions of office for government backbenchers. They hoped their recommendations would shift the balance in favour of the committees. Proposals included the possible remuneration of chairmen, a weekly half-hour debate devoted to a recent committee report and a small central staff unit specialising in public expenditure and pre-legislative scrutiny on which individual committees could call for support. Even if the committees were given more powers to order the production of documents, which the Liaison Committee postponed for future examination, the implementation of their proposals could not cure the lack of a separation of powers between the government and Parliament in the United Kingdom which is the root cause of the weakness of these committees in contrast to U.S. Congressional Committees. The tyranny of party has ensured that the committees have not altered the balance of power between the government and Parliament. The crux of the matter was summed up by Mr Cunningham, a rebellious right-wing Labour M.P. who later defected to the SDP, when he said, "In this place honourable Members often look for procedural prescriptions to ailments which are not procedural in nature but personal" (H.C. Deb., vol. 2, col. 1258, April 10, 1981). In other words the balance of power cannot be changed by improving procedures by select committees but by M.P.s using their votes.

THE HOUSE OF LORDS

The House of Lords, the second chamber of Parliament, is in a transitional stage. The Labour government elected in 1997 abolished the right of hereditary peers to be members of the House of Lords with the exception of 92 hereditary peers (House of Lords Act 1999, sections 1 and 2). This leaves a House consisting of nearly 700 members who are all life peers apart from the 26 bishops and archbishops and the remaining hereditary peers. The abolition of most of the hereditary peers was the first stage of the reform of the House of Lords. The second stage was initiated by the appointment of a Royal Commission to make recommendations about the role, functions and composition of the second chamber. It reported in January 2000 (Cm 4534). Its proposals have been debated in both Houses of Parliament (H.L. Deb. vol. 610, col. 910, March 7, 2000; H.C. Deb. vol. 352, col. 48 *et seq*, June 19, 2000) and subjected to much criticism but no consensus has emerged so far in favour of any blueprint for a reformed second chamber. Nevertheless, the government after being re-elected included reform of the House of Lords in the Queen's Speech (June 20, 2001). There have already been important changes in the appointment procedure of life peers and the way in which the interim House exercises its powers.

There were two major problems with the House of Lords as it existed before the House of Lords Act 1999; the first was the right to membership by virtue of inheritance, which is an anachronism in a modern democracy. Secondly and as a result of the former, there was a permanent Conservative majority in the Lords. This was not an overall majority of the House, because a substantial bloc of cross-benchers, who do not take a party whip, held the balance of power and contributed to the defeats which the Labour government elected in 1997 suffered at the hands of the hereditary peers.

The first stage of reform was aimed at these two anomalies but succeeded in perpetuating one of them. To prevent the House of Lords obstructing the Bill abolishing the rights of hereditary peers and other government legislation, the Labour government agreed to reprieve 92 hereditary peers until there was a fully reformed second chamber. Both sides gained from this victory of expediency over principle; the government got its Bill and the Opposition retained 92 hereditary peers, like a Trojan horse, to guarantee fundamental reform in the future.

Paradoxically this rump of hereditary peers can claim to be the only elected body in the House of Lords, as hereditary peers in each party group and the cross-benchers elected from their own members those who were to remain. Seventeen hereditary peers were also given life peerages, some because their titles were created in their life-times or they were former Leaders of the Lords. Important changes have been made in the appointment of life peers, who are created under the Life Peerages Act 1958 by the Queen on the advice of the Prime Minister. The government has established a non-statutory Appointments Commission for the interim House of Lords, consisting of an independent Chairman, three independent members and three nominees of the main political parties. They have advertised for applicants before making nominations for a number of cross-bench life-peers to the Prime Minister who recommends them to the Queen but the Prime Minister will still determine the number of life-peers to be appointed. As regards the life-peers who take the party whip, the Prime Minister will accept the nominees from other parties but will again determine the number to be appointed, so that he controls the party balance in the House. He has announced that Labour will seek parity with the Conservative Party in the House but not an overall majority. This parity had not been reached in June 2001 when there were over 200 Labour peers to nearly 230 Conservatives as well as over 60 Liberal Democrats and over 160 cross-benchers in a House of about 700 peers. This new composition of the interim House has had a profound effect on the exercise of its functions.

With the ejection of the vast majority of hereditary peers and, therefore, the in-built Conservative majority a new legitimacy has been claimed for the House of Lords, which is disputed by the government, because the House is not elected by the people. It was the lack of legitimacy of the House as formerly constituted which inhibited it from exercising its legal powers. Until 1911 all Bills had to have the consent of both the Lords and the Commons. The Prime Minister could ask the monarch to create sufficient peers in order to pass the legislation. It was this threat which enabled the great Reform Act 1832 to be passed. The threat was never put into practice (after 1712) but it played an important role in the constitutional crisis of 1909–11 when the House of Lords rejected the Liberal Government's budget proposals. After two General Elections in one year which were won by the Liberals and a promise by the King to create sufficient peers to force the House of Lords to agree to the curtailment of its powers, the Parliament Act 1911 was passed which abolished the veto of the House of Lords over Bills approved by the House of Commons, except for a Bill extending the life of Parliament beyond five years. This last provision gives the House of Lords the power to act as a constitutional long-stop. Instead of a veto the Lords were given a power to delay Bills for up to two years which was cut down to one year by the Parliament Act 1949. For Money Bills the period of delay is one month. The 1911 Act was only used three times to pass an Act, one of which was the Parliament Act 1949. The 1949 Act was used for the first time to pass the War Crimes Act 1991, though the House of Lords used its delaying power on a Trade Union Bill in 1975 but allowed it to pass when the Lords' consent was no longer necessary for it to become law.

The exercise of the legal power to delay Bills used to be hedged around with conventions. It was only to be used for issues of great constitutional or national importance to enable the government to think again and to allow public opinion to be mobilised. This convention was not observed by the Lords *vis-à-vis* the Labour governments from 1974–79 when they used their delaying power on a Trade Union Bill and refused to pass the Aircraft and Shipbuilding Industries Bill in 1976. The use of the delaying power for the War Crimes Bill was also outside the convention. This was a unique non party-political measure which had been passed through all its stages in the Commons on free votes. It was argued in the Lords that the Parliament Acts should only be used when the will of the government is frustrated by the Opposition using its majority in the House of Lords.

The second Bill to become law under the Parliament Act 1949, the European Parliamentary Elections Act 1999, was passed under very different circumstances. The Labour manifesto had promised to introduce proportional representation for the European Parliamentary elections but the system chosen, the closed party list system (where a vote is cast for a party), was criticised across the party-political spectrum. In the House of Lords at the last stage of the Bill an amendment was passed substituting the open list system, which enables a vote to be cast for a preferred candidate from the party list. This amendment "ping-ponged" between the two Houses an unprecedented five times before the Lords finally insisted on the amendment and the Bill was lost for the session. This precipitated the use of the Parliament Acts by the government in the next session, the Bill having been delayed for a year already.

Paradoxically, the Lords speeded it on its way by rejecting it at the Second Reading (the first stage of a Bill) on the second occasion, so that it could become law after one month. The later stages of the Bill mirrored the negotiations between the government and the Opposition peers about reform of the House of Lords, which later led to the reprieve of 92 hereditary peers and also to the collapse of opposition to this Bill by the Lords. The Bill was passed in unique circumstances but it provided a foretaste of things to come. The Earl of Onslow, one of its implacable opponents, drew the moral when he said that it provided a perfect example of why the House should be properly reformed. He added, "When it is properly reformed, we can use the powers that we have with legitimacy and pride rather than be blackmailed because we are told we are all idiots of hereditary peers" (H.L. Deb., vol. 594, col. 859, November 12, 1998).

Although the House of Lords has been only partly reformed it has flexed its muscles to an unprecedented extent. On February 22, 2000 (H.L. Deb. vol. 609, col. 136 *et seq*) the House of Lords broke with convention and by a big majority voted against an order made under the Greater London Authority Act 1999 concerned with the elections for the mayor of London. This was the first time this had happened since the Rhodesian Sanctions Order in 1968. The Lords have a veto over orders made under Acts of Parliament which have to be approved or can be annulled by both Houses of Parliament (see below), because the Parliament Acts do not apply to orders. Because the House is unelected there was a convention that the House would rarely vote against orders and the Opposition front-bench would abstain regardless of which party was in opposition. This convention was analogous to the famous Salisbury convention enunciated by the Leader of the Conservative Opposition in the Lords, after Labour's election victory in 1945. Under these rules the House of Lords would not reject or alter beyond recognition any Bill which had been in the government's manifesto at the General Election. It has been suggested by the present Leader of the Conservative Opposition in the Lords (Lord Strathclyde) that in the light of the new composition of the Lords this convention needs re-examination. However, the then Labour Leader of the House (Baroness Jay) rejected the proposal because the convention is based on the unelected nature of the House of Lords not on its party composition (H.L. Deb. vol. 608, col. 214, December 15, 1999).

These conflicting views have not yet been tested in the newly constituted House but the Lords have made ample use of their undoubted power of amendment. It is when the government are defeated in the Lords that they are seen as flexing their muscles. This reached its peak (over 350 defeats) during the Labour governments of 1974–79 which had a very small or no majority in the Commons. But it was also considerable, though much smaller, during the following 18 years of Conservative governments (242 defeats). It increased after Labour's election in 1997 (70 defeats in two sessions) and continued apace after the expulsion of the hereditary peers (36 defeats in one session). It is not so much the number of defeats which counts but the importance of the issue and whether the defeat is overturned by the government. On both these counts the defeats inflicted by the transitional House have been significant.

The government substantially accepted the defeat on the order relating to the election of the mayor of London by inserting a new Section 14 and Schedule 5 into the Representation of the People Bill 2000 providing for a free delivery of election addresses by the candidates, which was the principle at stake. Some of the most important defeats of the government by the transitional House of Lords have been on amendments to Bills which were first introduced in the Lords before passing to the Commons. The Parliament Acts cannot be used on such Bills, so that the government has to start a new Bill in the Commons if the Lords stand firm on their amendment. This happened when the government were overwhelmingly defeated by nearly 100 votes, including Labour peers, on an amendment to The Criminal Justice (Mode of Trial) Bill restricting a defendant's right to choose trial by jury (H.L. Deb. vol. 608, col. 1294, January 20, 2000). The government then abandoned the Bill and introduced a new and amended Bill in the House of Commons. This Bill was again defeated by a similar majority in the House of Lords on Second Reading (H L. vol. 616, col. 1033, September 28, 2000) but if it is reintroduced it can then become law under the Parliament Acts. On the equally controversial issue of repealing section 28 of the Local Government Act 1988 (outlawing the promotion of homosexuality by local authorities), which was contained in the Local Government Bill 2000, the government were again heavily defeated by a Conservative cross-party alliance including 15 Labour peers (H.L. Deb. vol. 609, col. 483, February 7, 2000). The government tried to reach a compromise through amendments to the Learning and Skills Bill 2000 providing for statutory guidelines on sex education. These amendments failed to placate the Lords and the repeal of section 28 was abandoned for the Parliament as the government did not wish to delay the Bill becoming law. The Parliament Acts could not be used for the Local Government Bill, which started in the Lords, and a new Bill could not become law without the consent of the Lords within the time-span of the Parliament.

In contrast the government has used the procedure under the Parliament Acts to lower the age of consent to homosexual acts to 16. This was not a manifesto commitment and was left to a free vote by M.P.s and peers. After its first rejection in the Lords on an amendment to the Crime and Disorder Bill 1998, the government introduced the Sexual Offences (Amendment) Bill 1998 in the Commons, including provisions which took account of some of the worries expressed in the House of Lords. When it reached the Lords it was rejected at the first stage (the Second Reading), the Salisbury convention was said not to be applicable, because the Bill was not in Labour's manifesto. The government in the next session invoked the Parliament Acts and again passed the Bill on a free vote. This time the Lords did not reject the Bill straight away (H.L. Deb. vol. 612, col. 167, April 11, 2000), but amended the Bill very late in the session (H.L. Deb., vol. 619, col. 19 *et seq.*, November 13, 2000). The government did not ask the House of Commons to consider these amendments before submitting the Bill for the Royal Assent under the Parliament Acts, the third Bill to become law under the Parliament Act 1949.

This resurgence of the House of Lords after the ejection of the hereditary peers was not unpredicted, though it was probably not intended by the government, who reiterate that nothing has changed in the relationship between the two Houses, which continues to be based on the pre-eminence of the House of Commons as the elected chamber. The maintaining of this position was written into the terms of reference of the Royal Commission on the Reform of the House of Lords. Starting from this premise and taking into account the other constitutional reforms enacted by the government, such as devolution to Scotland, Wales and Northern Ireland and the Human Rights Act 1998, the Commission resisted the temptation to recommend a more powerful second chamber and to radically alter the existing balance of power between the two Houses (Cm 4534, Chapter 3.15). The only changes to the powers of the second chamber they recommended were a minor change to the Parliament Acts to prevent their amendment without the consent of the second chamber (Chapter 5.15) and to reduce the veto power over orders made under Acts of Parliament to a delaying power (Chapter 7.37). This recommendation was based on the assertion that the veto power was not used in practice, an assumption which was proved false shortly after their report was published (*supra*). They also disagreed with those who argued that the Salisbury convention should not continue to bind a reformed second chamber and agreed with the government that it should be maintained because its philosophical underpinning was the pre-eminence of the House of Commons as the elected chamber (Chapter 4.21).

In a textbook illustration of a circular argument, the Commission later used the continuation of the Salisbury convention as an argument against an elected second chamber (Chapter 11.6). They regarded their terms of reference relating to the pre-eminence of the Commons as not only precluding a more powerful but also an elected second chamber. They rejected all the mechanisms for ensuring that a second elected House would not have equivalent electoral legitimacy with the Commons, such as more limited powers and elections at a different time, by a different system and for a different period. They also rejected a minority of non-elected members because it would create two classes of members (Chapter 11.7), an argument which did not prevent them from finally recommending an appointed second chamber with a minority of members elected on a regional basis by a system of proportional representation. The Commission could not agree on the number of elected members and proposed three models varying from 65 to 195 members in a chamber of about 550 members. The rest of the members should be selected by an independent Appointments Commission who would ensure that 20 per cent of members were not affiliated to one of the major political parties and that the political balance of the 80 per cent of politically affiliated members reflected the votes cast (not the seats won) at the last general election. This was to ensure that no single party would be likely to have a majority (Chapter 11.39).

The Royal Commission had a very mixed reception and seems to have pleased no-one apart from the government at whom its report seems to have been primarily aimed. There is no ideal solution to reform of the second chamber; it has been said that the problem basically is insoluble (Ian Gilmour, H.C. Deb. vol. 773, col. 1384, November 20, 1968). The aim is to create a more legitimate, independent and expert second chamber but these are conflicting ideals. Legitimacy in a democracy is best conferred by election, whilst independence from party politics and expertise imply appointment by an impartial body. To satisfy both criteria indicates a mixed chamber of elected and appointed members and, to achieve the correct balance, parity between the two types of members has been suggested. The big disadvantage of such a compromise solution, as of any proposal for a mixed chamber, is that there will be two classes of members who will not carry equal weight because of their different methods of selection.

Such a solution is an attempt to square the circle of giving the second chamber enough legitimacy to use its powers without threatening the pre-eminence of the House of Commons. Arguably this pre-eminence will be safeguarded by the continuation of the Parliament Acts, which limit the powers of the second chamber and the retention of the Salisbury convention, as recommended by the Royal Commission. The paradox is that a more legitimate second chamber is likely to have its legal powers (*e.g.* the veto power over orders) reduced because it will not feel so constrained in exercising them, as has been illustrated by the transitional House of Lords. A fully elected chamber, where elections take place at a different time and under a different system, so as not to produce a carbon copy of the Commons, is likely to feel even less restrained. Those who advocate this solution see the role of the second chamber as a counter-balance to the Executive's dominance over the House of Commons, which is the key to the elective dictatorship. This has not been redressed by any of the government's constitutional reforms.

3
ALLOCATION AND METHODS OF DECISION-MAKING I

PREROGATIVE POWERS

All decision-making powers of public authorities derive from Parliament with the exception of those derived from the preroga- tive. These are the residual powers of the Crown which derive from the common law. They include such important powers as declaring war, making treaties, dispatching the armed forces, *e.g.* sending the Task Force to the Falklands and even requisitioning merchant ships, including the QE 2, during the Falklands conflict (Requisitioning of Ships Order 1982). Because power derives from the prerogative the government does not need the authority of Parliament for the exercise of these powers, though in practice Parliament will be informed in such important cases, as hap- pened in the famous debate on Saturday, April 3, 1982 (H.C. Deb., vol. 21, col. 633) before the Task Force was dispatched to the Falklands. In the case of the Gulf War Parliament was recalled during the summer recess on September 6, 1990 (H.C. Deb., vol. 177, col. 734) to discuss the crisis after some British troops had already been dispatched. Another debate was held on January 15, 1991 (H.C. Deb., vol. 183, col. 734), the day on which the deadline for Iraq to comply with the UN resolution expired and before British troops went into action. Similarly, the instruction given by the Prime Minister prohibiting civil servants at the Government Communications Headquarters (GCHQ) from being members of a trade union, another illustration of a prerogative power, was announced to Parliament but only after it had been given, pre- sumably for reasons of national security (H.C. Deb., vol. 52, col. 917, January 25, 1984).

Nothing can illustrate better the enormous difference both legally and politically between the exercise of power by the gov- ernment under the prerogative instead of statute than the contro- versy surrounding ratification of the Treaty on European Union signed at Maastricht. The power of the government to agree and ratify international treaties is derived from the prerogative. The consent of Parliament is only required for those parts of the Treaty which need to be incorporated into U.K. law. This applied only to certain parts of the Maastricht Treaty. Parliament cannot amend a treaty, it can only refuse to enact it into domestic law. The critics of the Maastricht Treaty had to find ways to circumnavigate this rule by their amendments to the Bill (the European Communities (Amendment) Bill 1993)). The most controversial amendment concerned the Social Chapter, an agreement to implement the Social Charter concerned with the conditions of workers, which the U.K. had opted out of. The amendment to exclude the opt-out from the Bill was first said by the government to have the effect, if passed, of wrecking the treaty. After taking legal advice from the Attorney-General the government announced that it would have no legal effect and would not prevent ratification of the treaty, as it was, including the opt-out (H.C. Deb., vol. 219, col. 27 *et seq.*, February 15, 1993). They later accepted the amendment without a vote to deprive their opponents of an "entirely synthetic victory" (H.C. Deb., vol. 224, col. 207, May 5, 1993). The constitutional enormity of this stance was expressed succinctly by the opposition spokesman: "the Government would use the royal prerogative to ignore Parliament". (H.C. Deb., vol. 219, col. 29, February 15, 1993). However, the government's view was upheld by the court when it dismissed the action to prevent ratification of the Treaty brought by Lord Rees-Mogg (*R v. Foreign Secretary ex parte Rees-Mogg*, 1994).

Meanwhile the opposition had devised another mechanism to force the government's hand on the Social Chapter. They put forward a new clause which would prevent the Act coming into force until each House of Parliament had come to a Resolution on a motion considering the adoption of the Social Chapter. This clause, too, was finally accepted by the government without a vote, thereby pre-empting defeat (H.C. Deb., vol. 223, col. 529 *et seq.*, April 22, 1993). This was the time-bomb which exploded on July 22, 1993 (H.C. Deb., vol. 229, col. 608) when the House of Commons had a tied vote, later corrected to a majority of one (*ibid.* col. 623), against an opposition amendment to prevent the government ratifying the Treaty until it had notified its intention to adopt the Social Chapter. But it then defeated by eight votes the government motion to take note of the government's policy on opting-out of the Social Chapter, with 23 Conservative rebels voting against the government. This was immediately followed the next day by a motion which made the government's opt-out from the Social Chapter an issue of confidence, which the government won comfortably by 40 votes (H.C. Deb., vol. 229, col. 721, July 23, 1993). Instead of using the blunderbuss of the royal prerogative to ratify the Treaty with the opt-out against the wishes of the House of Commons, it had to use the nuclear deterrent of a confidence motion.

DELEGATED LEGISLATION

Parliament can make only a limited number of decisions in the form of legislation. Acts of Parliament should lay down the principles but their detailed implementation has to be delegated to ministers. The Act will give power to a minister to make regulations, called statutory instruments, for this purpose, *i.e.* rules drafted in his Department which the Act may provide shall be laid before Parliament either for approval or for annulment. In the former case the government has to provide time to debate the instruments for at least one and a half hours, though in some important cases more time has been allowed for debate. In the case of annulment M.P.s, normally from the opposition, have to put down a prayer and debates are held after 10 p.m. and are cut off at 11.30 p.m. The vote, which is now deferred to a later day (see below, Conclusion), will normally be a foregone conclusion. Of the over three thousand statutory instruments which are now made every year the vast majority are not subject to parliamentary approval and only a small number of prayers are debated late at night. There is thus little opportunity to debate statutory instruments on the floor of the House and no possibility of amending them unless a minister can be persuaded to withdraw the instrument and bring it back in a different form. It is now possible for statutory instruments to be debated in a standing committee but they have to return to the House to be approved or annulled there. The three standing committees which have been set up for the consideration of proposals for European Community legislation made by the institutions of the European Community can question a minister before debating the document.

The lack of parliamentary scrutiny is inherent in the use of statutory instruments, as they are intended to save parliamentary time. So long as they deal with the nuts and bolts of legislation this is acceptable. There is, however, a growing tendency to use statutory instruments for matters of policy and principle which should be embodied in the Act itself. Thus the Education (Student Loans) Act 1990 is effectively nothing more than an authorisation for the Secretary of State for Education to make arrangements for enabling students to receive loans towards their maintenance whilst attending courses of higher education. Such framework or skeleton Acts which may contain over 100 regulation-making powers, as in the Child Support Act 1991, are becoming increasingly common. While such Acts may be acceptable in time of war or emergency such as the Emergency Powers (Defence) Act 1939, they fundamentally alter the balance of power between Parliament and the executive, particularly when the subordinate legislation is subject to little or sometimes no parliamentary oversight.

The Scott Report castigated one of the worst examples of such an Act, namely the Import, Export and Customs Powers (Defence) Act 1939. This Act which was rushed through Parliament at the beginning of the war, enabled the government to prohibit the import and export of any goods under import and export control orders which were subject to no parliamentary oversight whatsoever. The Act remained in force long after the war ended until 1990, when the war-time powers were made permanent under the Import and Export Control Act 1990. This Act perpetuated the lack of parliamentary control, due to cynical negotiations with the Opposition, which Sir Richard Scott chronicled in lurid detail. He commented that Parliamentary supervision should not have been treated as an optional extra and that this cavalier attitude supported the charge that the Constitution had become an elective dictatorship (H.C. 115 (1995–96), Section C). Finally, in December 1999, the Labour government elected to lay export control orders before Parliament for information but only new legislation can enable Parliament to take action on them (H.C. 225 (1999–2000), para. 4). However, four departmental select committees acting jointly now give detailed scrutiny to the annual reports on arms exports and have recommended a system of Parliamentary scrutiny before export licences are granted (H.C. 212 (2000–2001)). This has so far not been accepted by the government but the committees have been promised confidential briefings on general policy considerations and the Export Control Bill was published in June 2001, which gives Parliament the right to scrutinise export control orders and specifies the purposes of export controls. When this Bill finally comes into force the Scott Report will at last have been implemented (H.C. Deb., vol. 359, col. 1WH, December 14, 2000).

The most criticised form of delegation is that which gives ministers powers by regulation to amend an Act of Parliament, called Henry VIII clauses. All these developments have given rise to much concern in Parliament and in particular in the House of Lords, which has resulted in the setting up there of a new committee. The Delegated Powers and Deregulation Committee scrutinises every government Bill as to whether it inappropriately delegates legislative power or provides for an inappropriate degree of parliamentary scrutiny and reports to the Lords before the Committee stage. Skeleton Bills and Henry VIII clauses are prime targets for report. The Committee made a damning report on part of the Education Bill 1994 dealing with student unions because it was a "skeleton bill" and interfered with the freedom of association of students (H.L. 11, 1993–94). These provisions were later dropped from the Bill (H.L. Deb., vol. 552, col. 57, *Written Answers*, February 24, 1994). Similarly, the government accepted the strictures of the Committee and made amendments to the Pollution Prevention and Control Bill 1999, which was characterised as a skeleton Bill, that is little more than a licence to legislate. This was only the fourth time the Committee had attached this label to a whole Bill (H.L. 112 (1998–99) para. 23). Where the Committee has recommended that provisions should be put in the Bill itself rather than be implemented through regulations or that statutory instruments should be subject to approval rather than annulment, this has mostly if not invariably been accepted by governments. It is paradoxical that it is the unelected House of Lords rather than the House of Commons which set up this committee which functions as "the constitutional conscience of the House in relation to delegated powers". The House of Lords is here performing its important function of acting as constitutional watchdog.

The most far-reaching provisions for delegated legislation are contained in the Deregulation and Contracting Out Act 1994 which gives power to a minister to make orders to amend or repeal any Act which imposes an unnecessary burden on a trade, business or profession, where the burden can be removed or reduced without removing any necessary protection. The Act was criticised as a constitutional outrage in the House of Lords and as unprecedented in time of peace. This is in marked contrast with its operation in practice which has been infrequent and uncontroversial. This is the result partly of the procedure for making such orders and partly because of the content of the orders which have been put forward. Only one order, the Sunday Dancing and Licensing Order has run into serious controversy before being approved in an amended form (H.C. 37 (2000–01)). Nearly all suggested amendments have been accepted by governments and there have been no debates on an order on the Floor of the House of Commons.

This illustrates the success of the procedure which has been adopted for approval of deregulation orders. The Act provides for a two-stage procedure. A draft of the order has to be laid before both Houses for 60 days and is considered within the time by the Deregulation Committee of the House of Commons and the Delegated Powers Committee in the House of Lords. Amendments are then made in the order to take account of the committees' recommendations before the order is laid before both Houses for approval. As a result, when the committees consider the draft order a second time, the problems have been solved and approval becomes a formality.

It has been suggested by successive Procedure Committees of the House of Commons that the same procedure should be adopted for a small number of very important and complex orders and this has already happened in the case of remedial orders under the Human Rights Act 1998, section 10, which can amend an Act of Parliament declared incompatible with the European Convention on Human Rights. So deregulation orders have been transformed from constitutional pariahs into rôle models. The Regulatory Reform Act 2001 extends the ambit of the 1994 Act and repeals and replaces it.

Whilst at one end of the spectrum statutory instruments are being used for provisions which should be contained in Acts of Parliament, at the other end statutory instruments are being replaced by codes of practice, codes of conduct, guidelines, circulars and a miscellany of rules which have been given the title of "quasi-legislation". Unlike statutory instruments, this material has varying degrees of legal force. Its legal effect will depend on the Act under which it is made. The Highway Code is probably the first illustration of this development. Breach of the code is not a criminal offence but it can be taken into account in any criminal or civil proceedings (Road Traffic Act 1988, section 38). This provision has been used in an increasing number of areas ranging from health and safety at work, industrial relations and race relations, to education and police custody. The main reason for using codes with limited legal effect in preference to legal regulations was a preference for the voluntary approach. In these situations it was thought that persuasion would be more effective than compulsion and codes would be more advisory and persuasive than legal regulation. They also have the practical advantage of not having to be couched in precise legal language and they can also be more flexible. However, their flexibility will depend very much on the procedural safeguards which regulate their making and approval. Here there are a plethora of different provisions in the parent Acts but certain standard control mechanisms recur in many statutes. There is often provision for consultation with affected interests, parliamentary approval or the opportunity for annulment and publication. The difficulty of locating this material, because publication takes such diverse forms, has been one of the main criticisms of these mechanisms for laying down rules from the beginning of this development.

Quasi-legislation is used to regulate the conduct not only of private individuals but also of public authorities. The codes of practice made under the Police and Criminal Evidence Act 1984 may be regarded as a prototype. These lay down the way in which the police should exercise their functions under the Act in much more detail than the Act itself. Breach of the codes does not render the police liable to criminal or civil proceedings, though it must be taken into account in such proceedings where relevant (section 67). Similar provisions are now contained in statutes concerned with local government and provide for codes directed to local authorities. The novelty lies in embodying in Acts of Parliament provisions for such codes of guidance to local authorities. Until recently such guidance, usually contained in circulars from a government department to local authorities, was provided without any statutory provisions. The circulars, often a mixture of explanation and advice, were used in some cases as a substitute for legislation because the government preferred persuasion to legal regulation of local authorities. Thus circulars were used by the Labour government in 1965 to implement its policy for comprehensive education, and legislation was only used as a last resort to bring a few recalcitrant authorities to heel in 1976.

There is still a vast number of rules and guidelines which have no statutory basis but may have some legal force. Planning policy is often contained in guidance notes which have to be taken into account when making planning decisions. The most common examples are internal rules of government departments which structure the way they exercise their discretion. The most controversial recent examples were the Howe guidelines which laid down the criteria for dealing with export licences for arms to Iraq. Much of the Scott Report was devoted to their criticism. They had no statutory authority, were not subject to parliamentary scrutiny, they could be changed at will and were published after a year's delay, though they did not have to be published at all (H.C. 115 (1995–96) section D)). They illustrate the worst aspects of such rules, the lack of certainty and insufficient control mechanisms.

INTERPRETATION AND APPLICATION OF LEGISLATION AND DELEGATED LEGISLATION

Tribunals

Rules, whether laid down in an Act or in regulations made under an Act, have to be interpreted and applied to individual cases. Interpretation of statutes and statutory instruments is a matter for the courts but Acts of Parliament may entrust this function to other bodies, though, as we shall see, these will themselves be subject to the supervision of the courts. In an increasing number of areas tribunals have been preferred to courts as decision-making bodies. There are some 2,000 tribunals covering such diverse areas as social security, immigration, employment, taxation, and the national health service. The reasons for preferring tribunals to courts are both practical and ideological.

Tribunals do not consist of lawyers, though increasingly the chairman is a lawyer appointed by the Lord Chancellor. The other members may be representatives of interest groups, *e.g.* employers or employees in the case of employment tribunals, or they may have a particular expertise, *e.g.* doctors in the case of mental health tribunals. When some of the tribunals were first set up after 1945 it was made explicit by the government that the courts were not trusted to decide disputes in certain areas of social policy such as national insurance, rent and the national health service. Later criticism centred on the members of tribunals being drawn from a narrow social spectrum and being unfamiliar with the problems of the people appearing before them, particularly in the case of supplementary benefit appeal tribunals. It has also been alleged that in certain cases tribunals have been used to give the appearance of impartiality to the implementation of controversial policies. This allegation has been made particularly against the forerunners of social security tribunals and immigration tribunals (Harlow and Rawlings, 1997, p. 462 *et seq.*). The policies are embodied in the Acts and regulations or rules made under them, the tribunals can only interpret and apply them. If ministers do not approve of the interpretation in a particular case, it can always be reversed by changing the law. Ministers cannot interfere directly in individual cases but they have been known not to publicise unfavourable decisions so as to limit their impact, or to settle test cases in order to prevent an unfavourable decision. Tribunals were firmly categorised as part of the machinery for adjudication rather than administration by the Franks Committee which was asked to investigate the constitution and working of tribunals in 1957 (Cmnd. 218). To achieve impartiality, which was one of its aims for tribunals, it recommended that members should be neither appointed nor dismissed by ministers. This was only partly implemented so that chairmen are usually appointed by the Lord Chancellor or from a panel of members appointed by him, and all members can normally be removed only by him. As most members hold office only for a limited period, this latter safeguard is not very significant.

The practical advantages of tribunals are procedural. In general they are cheaper, quicker and more informal than courts, though the variations between tribunals are as great as their differences from the courts. Some, like the Lands Tribunal, are indistinguishable from a court in all but name, whilst in a social security tribunal all the participants, including the members of the tribunal, may sit round a table. In between these extremes of formality, the members of an employment tribunal may sit on a raised dais with the parties sitting at tables in front of them. Procedure varies accordingly from an almost informal conversation round the table to a full-scale hearing with the parties represented by lawyers and evidence on oath. Legal aid is not available for representation before almost all tribunals and many applicants, therefore, appear in person or may not appear at all in the case of social security tribunals. Some see the remedy for this in making legal aid or other representation more widely available, so that the parties are more evenly matched. Alternatively, it is possible to see the members of tribunals playing a more active role in the proceedings, as many do in practice, by asking questions and bringing out the salient issues. There is also evidence that applicants prefer to play a more active role in the proceedings rather than listening passively to their lawyer present their case (Bell, 1975, p. 16). Neither of these remedies affects the outcome of proceedings as much as specialist representation (Genn, 1993). If tribunals are too closely modelled on courts they lose the procedural advantages which were the main justification for their creation. On the other hand, they must be seen to be fair and independent from the government department concerned if they are to be trusted by the citizen.

Latterly there has been an increasing trend to substitute the principles of economy, efficiency and expedition for the ideals of openness, fairness and impartiality advocated by the Franks Committee. This has resulted in the provision of internal review procedures within a government department or agency instead of an appeal to an independent tribunal. The most striking example is the use of this procedure for refusals of lump sum benefits under the Social Fund to recipients of income support. Formerly an appeal lay to a tribunal in this type of case. This trend has been deplored by the Council on Tribunals which is the statutory watchdog overseeing the working of tribunals (H.C. 64, 1990–91).

The streamlining of decision-making has continued to accelerate especially in the area of social security. Applicants now have to specifically ask for an oral hearing, otherwise the case will be dealt with purely on the papers. In addition the Labour government adopted most of the previous government's proposals for reform of social security adjudication and substituted a tribunal consisting of a legally qualified member sitting alone for a three person tribunal including two lay members in mainstream (*i.e.* non-medical) social security appeals. This was implemented by regulations (Social Security and Child Support (Decisions and Appeals) Regulations 1999) rather than by the Social Security Act 1998, thus avoiding detailed parliamentary scrutiny. It was only through an amendment by the Chairman of the Council on Tribunals, whilst the Bill was passing through the Lords, that it was ensured that the single member sitting as a tribunal would be legally qualified — a neat illustration of the use and evasion of Parliamentary scrutiny.

Ministers

Ministers entrust to courts, tribunals or any other independent body those individual decisions which they do not wish to take themselves, though they usually reserve the power to lay down the policies to be applied by such bodies. The rationale behind such allocation is very varied and by no means consistent either between governments of different party political complexions or even between those of the same political colour. Thus the Labour opposition opposed giving wide discretionary powers to the Restrictive Practices Court to determine whether restrictive trade agreements were against the public interest. On the other hand a subsequent Labour government entrusted wide discretionary powers to immigration tribunals when determining immigration appeals, which was opposed by the then Conservative opposition. In contrast, governments of both parties have refused to entrust decisions about the provision of grants to assist industry to a court or tribunal, even where detailed criteria were laid down by statute, because they wished to reserve questions of interpretation to themselves. Again, governments of both parties may agree to give wide discretionary powers to an independent body so as to eliminate political considerations, *e.g.* the allocation of licences by the Independent Television Commission. When governments want to take into account their own policy in reaching a decision and do not want to entrust its interpretation to another body, they will reserve the decisions to themselves, though in practice only the most controversial cases will be decided by ministers personally. The rest will be decided by civil servants in the Department, the level at which the decision is made depending on its importance.

Where decisions are made by government departments in the name of the minister the procedure may be completely informal. This is the position with regard to grants to assist industry. These are negotiated between the applicant and officials in the Department who interpret the statutory provisions and internal guidelines which supplement them. A firm which may be disadvantaged by the granting of assistance to a rival concern has no opportunity to object. Governments have rejected all attempts by M.P.s to formalise these procedures, though applicants are given guidance about the criteria that the Department uses. Governments have insisted on retaining the maximum flexibility for these potentially politically sensitive decisions, refusing to be bound by any appeal mechanism or outside advisory body.

Public inquiries. In marked contrast to this informal decision-making process for decisions which can involve the public expenditure of millions of pounds is the elaborate public inquiry procedure which is obligatory for a vast number of decisions varying from the appeal against a refusal of planning permission to the building of roads, airports and nuclear power stations. It is revealing that the same basic procedure is prescribed for such widely disparate decisions, whose only common feature is that they involve interference with private land and that their origin lies in the private Act of Parliament which at one time had to be passed before these rights could be taken away compulsorily. The procedure for passing such Acts, which were used for the building of the railways and canals involves a judicial-type hearing before a small committee in each House. This procedure gave rise to much controversy in the 1980s because it was used for some highly politically controversial Bills, in particular Bills to expand private ports to enable the importation of foreign coal which led to the closure of British pits. M.P.s also resented the use of private Bills to by-pass planning procedures, as happened in the case of the Lyndhurst Bypass Bill (H.C. 650, 1987–88). After a report from a Joint Committee of both Houses (H.L. 97, 1987–88) the Transport and Works Act 1992 provided that a minister could authorise railway and tramway schemes by statutory instruments after hearing objections at a public local inquiry. If he considers the scheme to be of national significance the approval of both Houses of Parliament is necessary before the proposal can proceed to a public inquiry. Thus Parliament has divested itself of more powers and delegated them to ministers but it has also recognised that the public local inquiry is a better mechanism for public participation than Parliament itself.

A public local inquiry is held before an inspector appointed by the minister who conducts the inquiry and reports to the minister. He, or in most cases his officials, then makes the decision, usually without any parliamentary involvement. The public inquiry procedure still performs its original function of protecting landowners in the run-of-the-mill appeal by an applicant against refusal of planning permission by a local authority. In most of these cases the power to make the decision is now vested in the inspector, which in practice means that they are made by a different type of official, as few decisions reach the minister himself. In most cases the applicant now opts for an informal written procedure but he has the statutory right to a full oral hearing. The Council on Tribunals fought a successful battle to prevent the removal or watering down of this right by the Planning and Compensation Act 1991 (Council on Tribunals Report for 1990–91). This proposal formed part of a package of provisions in the Act to streamline the planning system in the interests of efficiency. Again we see the pursuit of speed and economy at the expense of fairness.

At an inquiry the main protagonists are no longer just the local authority who refused permission and the applicant for such permission, but third parties, *e.g.* neighbours and those concerned with the wider environment who, though they have no legal rights, are allowed to state their views to the inquiry and whose representations may be taken into account. This has turned many such inquiries into contests between private land-owners rather than resolving conflicts between the private and public interest, though the public interest is only an amalgam of private interests. A neighbourhood is merely a collection of neighbours. As has been said elsewhere, one man's property is another man's environment (Ganz, 1974, p. 55).

The judicialisation of inquiries received a strong impetus from the Franks Committee (Cmnd. 218, 1957) which was asked to investigate the procedure of inquiries as well as tribunals. It made many recommendations, which were mostly implemented, to make the procedure more like a court hearing than an administrative procedure designed to inform the minister. Reasons now have to be given for decisions and the inspector's report has to be published, and the minister cannot disagree with his findings except on matters of policy without giving the parties further opportunities to make representations or reopening the inquiry. As a result, inquiries have become more court-like with parties represented by lawyers, adopting courtroom techniques of cross-examination before an inspector whose judicial appearance Franks wanted enhanced by putting his appointment into the hands of the Lord Chancellor. This has not been implemented, except many years later in the case of motorway inquiries, but the natural corollary of these developments has been to turn the inspector into the judge who makes the decision in the case of most planning appeals which are not politically controversial. The controversial cases can always be called-in for decision by the minister and it is in these major inquiries into projects such as the building of a third London airport, a fifth terminal at Heathrow airport or a new type of nuclear power station at Sizewell or, to a lesser extent, the building of motorways that most problems have been encountered in adapting the highly judicialised public inquiry procedure as a prelude to important political decisions.

By widening the terms of reference of the inquiry to investigate the need for the project, in addition to its siting at a particular place and by adding expert assessors to assist the inspector, who can commission his own research, the inquiry has been broadened into an investigation of major political and economic issues such as the desirability of nuclear power or airports policy. This examination takes place within the straitjacket of a court-like procedure with the major participants represented by high-powered lawyers. The inspector's report and recommendations are made to the minister and the ultimate decision in such important cases may well be made at Cabinet level. The inspector's recommendations, reached after years of investigation, may be overturned for purely political reasons, as happened to the recommendations of the Roskill Inquiry into the siting of the third London airport in 1971. Parliament has as a rule no legal role to play in these decisions, which it has conferred on ministers, but recently it has insisted on debating the issues before decisions are made. This has involved difficult contortions so as not to fall foul of the legal provisions relating to the handling of the inspector's report by the minister. All these difficulties epitomise the problem of reaching a political decision through a judicial procedure.

There have been a number of attempts to grapple with this problem. A two-stage procedure has been suggested, where the first stage would be inquisitorial and investigate the policy issues, such as the need for the project, and the second stage would be a public inquiry into the siting of the project. There is already statutory provision for such a two-stage process in the Town and Country Planning Act 1990, (section 101) but it has never been used because of the difficulty of separating the policy issues at stage 1 from the site-specific issues at stage 2. The latest attempt to solve this problem is a proposal to introduce a procedure modelled on the Transport and Works Act 1992, under which Parliament would approve the broad principle of a major project and the subsequent inquiry would deal with detailed and local matters. The sting in the tail would be that the inquiry at stage 2 could not discuss matters approved by Parliament at stage 1 (Streamlining the processing of major projects through the planning system, May 1999, Department of Environment, Transport and the Regions). The proposal to preclude discussion at stage 2 has already been criticised by the Council on Tribunals (H.C. 30 (1999–2000) para. 2.176–2.177) and would be just as unworkable as the procedure under the Town and Country Planning Act 1990. Nevertheless parliamentary approval could strengthen the inspector's hand in curtailing discussion, as could the proposal to publish statements of national policy relating to major projects before they are considered at a public inquiry. The decision-making process following a public inquiry could have been thrown into disarray if a High Court decision, which declared certain planning decisions made by the Secretary of State to be incompatible with the rights enshrined in the Human Rights Act 1998, had been upheld on appeal (see below, Chapter 6).

In stark contrast to these public inquiry procedures for major projects is the use of the hybrid Bill procedure for authorising the building of the Channel Tunnel. The same procedure has been employed for the construction of the Channel Tunnel rail link. A hybrid Bill is a government Bill, which has a committee stage like a private Bill, where a small committee hears objectors who can show an interest affected by the Bill in accordance with strict criteria laid down by each House. The committee cannot question the principle of building the project which is decided when the Bill gets a second reading. The use of this procedure for authorising the Channel Tunnel in 1986–87 was strongly criticised because it was much quicker and gave less scope for objections to be heard than a major public inquiry which may last for years. These criticisms echo those made by members of both Houses about private Bill procedure and illustrate how far we have moved in this area from a representative to a participatory democracy, where individual citizens and pressure groups expect to be consulted.

Consultation and open government. The consultation of affected interest groups before decisions are made by the government is well established in certain areas but is by no means universal. Acts of Parliament are normally preceded by consultation with those affected, though this may be very cursory and without any noticeable effect (*Making the Law*, Hansard Society, 1992, Chapter 3). Bills are often preceded by consultation papers, followed by White Papers setting out the government's proposals on which further consultation takes place before the Bill is drafted. Both types of document may also be debated in Parliament. As we have seen, some Bills have been published in draft form and been scrutinised by Parliamentary committees before being introduced in Parliament. Similar procedures may be used for delegated legislation. Some town planning regulations have been preceded by consultation papers and the Highway Code has been through such a consultation stage. Consultation on statutory instruments which may go through many drafts is now the norm, though this is rarely provided for by statute. In the case of statutory codes of practice there is frequently a duty to consult affected interests embodied in the statute. Even non-statutory circulars have been subjected to intensive consultation, such as the circular dealing with green belts round built-up areas. There have also been startling examples of the lack of consultation, such as the instruction by Mrs Thatcher prohibiting employees at the secret Government Communications Headquarters from being members of trade unions, which the courts would have held to be unlawful but for the considerations of national security involved (*Council of Civil Service Unions v. Minister for the Civil Service*, 1984). It has even been held by the Court of Appeal that a non-statutory circular on immigration by the Home

Secretary could not be changed without giving an applicant in receipt of the circular an opportunity to make representations (*R. v. Home Secretary ex parte Asif Khan*, 1984). But it is doubtful whether this case can be applied generally to changes of policy by which individuals are deleteriously affected (*R v. Ministry of Defence, ex parte Walker*, 2000). In a case where there were statutory provisions for consultation of those affected by the regulations, the court held that it was unfair in the circumstances not to show them the advice of independent experts on which the regulations were based and quashed the regulations (*R. v. Health Secretary, ex parte U.S. Tobacco*, 1991).

Consultation may be institutionalised by making it obligatory to consult an advisory body, as is the case with social security regulations. It is also now becoming more common for the departmental select committees to consider regulations, codes of practice and even circulars before they are debated in the House of Commons or reach their final form. Such committees also examine policy statements from the government which may be contained in White Papers and preceded by consultation papers. Both consultation papers and White Papers may invite further comments from the public, though this is more usual with the former than the latter. Draft policy statements may also be used for this purpose. There is enormous variation in the extent to which the policy-making process by the government is open to public debate. The review of the supplementary benefits scheme by a team of officials in the Department of Health and Social Security in 1978 (Social Assistance) was not only published but members of the team answered questions at meetings throughout the country. This was a rather exceptional exercise in open government. Though there was a general directive by the Head of the Civil Service in 1978 to publish factual background material to policy studies unless ministers decided otherwise (H.C. Deb., vol. 942, col. 691, *Written Answers*, January 26, 1978), a later Head of the Civil Service stated that the reasons for deciding against publication might often be nothing more weighty than political embarrassment (Wass, 1983). The degree of political embarrassment which can be caused by exposing the policy-making process to public view was nowhere better illustrated than during the Westland affair when Cabinet meetings and confidential departmental meetings were openly discussed in Parliament and the media. These revelations pale into insignificance beside those made to the Scott inquiry into the Matrix Churchill Affair. The leaking of confidential letters written by ministers and civil servants is now commonplace.

These frequent leaks can be seen as symptoms of a system of closed government. Mr Major's government took some steps towards more openness such as the publication of the committees of the Cabinet (H.C. Deb., vol. 208, col. 110, *Written Answers*, May 19, 1992) and the publication of a Memorandum of Guidance, "Questions of Procedure for Ministers" (now the ministerial Code of Conduct, Cabinet office, 1997), which was hitherto secret. He even appointed a minister with responsibility for open government as well as the Citizen's Charter (now Service First). The latter provides for the publication of much information such as performance targets and league tables of performance. All this falls far short of a legal right for the citizen to obtain government documents subject to specific exceptions.

In 1994, the Conservative government issued a Code of Practice committing government departments to publishing facts and analyses of facts considered relevant in framing major policy proposals when the decisions are announced, giving reasons for administrative decisions and meeting reasonable requests for information relating to policies, actions and decisions of departments. There are the usual exemptions for information which would harm national security, defence, law enforcement, the economy, personal privacy and confidentiality and for internal policy advice. There have been several thousands of requests for information and about 40 complaints annually to the Parliamentary Commissioner for Administration (Ombudsman) (see below Chapter 5) to whom complaints can be made if information is withheld in breach of the Code. He can recommend disclosure so that enforcement is by persuasion.

The Conservative government explicitly rejected the courts or a tribunal as enforcement mechanisms on the grounds that this would be too rigid and would delegate political decisions to appointed judges. In other words ministers were not prepared to give up having the last word in this sensitive area. This is the fundamental difference between a statutory "right to know" and the Code of Practice. The Labour government finally grasped this nettle, having committed itself in its manifesto to legislation on freedom of information. Implementing this pledge encountered many vicissitudes. A White Paper (Cm 3818) was issued in December 1997 to general acclaim. It proposed a legal right of access to records or information from a vast number of public bodies ranging from government departments, health authorities, public corporations to local authorities, schools and universities. Though the Security Services were to be completely excluded from the legislation, the exempted categories of information were carefully delimited. They covered the areas of national security, defence, international relations, law enforcement, privacy and commercial confidentiality and policy advice. In each case, except the last, the test for exemption was whether disclosure could cause substantial harm to the interest concerned. Only in the case of policy advice did the harm not have to be substantial. The final decision on whether these tests were satisfied and whether disclosure must be made was entrusted to an Information Commissioner with legal powers to order disclosure.

Euphoria over the White Paper did not last long. The minister in charge of freedom of information, who was located in the Cabinet Office, was sacked and the issue was transferred to the Home Office. A draft Bill emerged in May 1999 and was heavily criticised by Committees in both Houses of Parliament (H.C. 570 (1998–99) and H.L. 97 (1998–99)). An amended Bill was introduced in the House of Commons in November 1999 and was further amended in its passage through Parliament. Controversy centred on the fundamental distinction between a legal right of access to information, subject to specific exemptions, policed by an independent arbiter with legal powers of enforcement and access to information through voluntary disclosure. The Freedom of Information Act 2000, unlike the White Paper, comes closer to enshrining the latter rather than the former.

The difference stems from the width of the exemptions contained in the Act which uses the term prejudice instead of substantial harm and in a number of cases exempts information by category or class rather than with reference to the harm likely to be caused by disclosure. This is particularly controversial in the case of the exemption for information relating to the formulation of government policy (section 35). To what extent this covers factual background information as well as policy advice has been much discussed but the government steadfastly refused to exclude factual information from the exemption and preferred to deal with the issue in the context of disclosure in the public interest.

To counter-balance these wide exemptions the Act provides for disclosure by a public authority of exempt information (with some exceptions) unless the public interest in maintaining the exemption outweighs the public interest in disclosure (section 2). In particular, regard must be had to the public interest in the disclosure of factual background information when considering the exemption relating to the formulation of government policy. The crucial difference with respect to disclosure in the public interest of exempt information is that the Information Commissioner does not have the final say over a refusal to disclose. The government made several concessions on this issue until only a Cabinet minister or the Attorney-General can override the Information Commissioner's decision ordering disclosure (section 53). Nevertheless, the compromise illustrates the government's final reluctance in sensitive areas to submit its judgements on the public interest in the disclosure of information to an independent arbiter or even to approval by Parliament, though the minister's veto has to be laid before Parliament.

4

ALLOCATION AND METHODS OF DECISION-MAKING II

QUANGOS AND NATIONALISED INDUSTRIES

A mechanism for consultation which has flourished since 1997 is the task force, over 300 having been set up to provide policy advice and make recommendations to the government in specific areas ranging from football to the New Deal for the unemployed. These working parties are appointed by ministers entirely ad hoc and are intended to last less than two years, though some have survived longer and some have been reclassified as more formal advisory bodies. In contrast with the latter, there are no rules for appointments to or procedures to be observed by such bodies nor any external body to oversee them. Their membership covers a wide range of interests including producers, consumers, experts and trade unionists. Their reports are published, though their deliberations and research work would probably be exempted from disclosure under the Freedom of Information Act as falling under the formulation of government policy. These temporary advisory bodies shade imperceptibly into a much larger and more permanent category of public bodies which has proliferated under all governments.

Where governments want to take decisions out of the political arena but do not want to entrust them to the courts or tribunals, they can allocate them to a public body set up for this purpose. These bodies can be loosely described as quasi-autonomous non-governmental organisations (quangos). They can be used for very different purposes and set up by governments of opposite political persuasions. Some exist with all-party agreement, others are subject to acute political controversy. At some times they are very much in fashion, at other times severely under attack, and these fluctuations cut across party lines. The Labour government after 1945 set up public corporations to run the nationalised industries or non-commercial services such as the New Town Development Corporations. Mr Heath's Conservative government in 1970 followed the advice of the Fulton Committee on the Civil Service (Cmnd. 3638, 1968) to hive off activities from the civil service for reasons of managerial efficiency. Mrs Thatcher waged war on quangos as symbols of patronage, bureaucracy and public expenditure but this did not prevent her from creating new ones where she thought it necessary, such as the urban development corporations for London's Docklands and other inner city areas and the boards which took over some of the functions of the GLC and Metropolitan County Councils which were abolished by the Local Government Act 1985. Some of these bodies now fall within the remit of the mayor of London (see below). Some bodies like the BBC, the Independent Television Commission and the Arts Council have been generally recognised as useful buffers protecting the area in question from direct political interference. On the other hand, the National Enterprise Board and its predecessor, the Industrial Reorganisation Corporation, set up by Labour governments to give assistance to industry, were each axed by the succeeding Conservative governments because they were not politically acceptable. Quangos are neither good nor bad, the basic question is to what extent it is desirable that decisions should be distanced from political considerations and be taken by experts applying commercial, artistic or professional criteria.

There are no clear guidelines about when this is desirable but there are some functions which are better carried out at arm's length from the elected government, such as regulatory and commercial activities and the funding of the arts, science and higher education bodies. The Labour government pledged that it would not create new quangos unless it was the most cost-effective and appropriate means of carrying out the function and there are quinquennial reviews to examine whether an existing quango should continue in existence. There has been little change in the total number of quangos since the 1997 General Election (H.C. 367 (2000–01, para. 8)). These bodies are notoriously difficult to map, as there is no single definition for the huge array of appointed bodies which perform public functions. They can be broadly divided into Non-Departmental Public Bodies (NDPBs) which perform public functions at the national level at arm's length from ministers. These number about 800 and can be subdivided into those carrying out executive and advisory functions. In addition there are the National Health Service bodies such as NHS Trusts and Local Public Spending Bodies including universities and former grant-maintained schools. The executive NDPBs alone spent £24 billion between 1999–2000.

The abolition of many of these bodies is not now regarded as a realistic option and a Parliamentary committee found it difficult to think of any specific body where it would be desirable to have clear political control and more direct ministerial accountability (H.C. 209 (1998–99) para. 28). The corollary of independence from political control is lack of democratic accountability. Consequently debate has concentrated on other mechanisms of accountability such as openness and making appointments subject to external scrutiny. Controversy has focused on the appointments system, where both major parties have been guilty of cronyism by appointing their supporters. Since the setting-up of the Committee on Standards in Public Life, guidelines have been drawn up for such appointments, including appointment on merit, external assessors and oversight of the system by the Commissioner for Public Appointments. These have not, however, prevented accusations of political appointments to NHS bodies by the Commissioner and further safeguards such as an independent appointments commission have been suggested (H.C. 410 (1999–2000 para. 49). This has been implemented. Politically appointed quangos represent the worst of both worlds; they do not take decisions out of politics but they are not democratically accountable. In other words they exercise political power without political responsibility.

These questions have been most hotly debated in the case of the nationalised industries. When the majority of the nationalised industries were created after 1945, the model adopted was the arm's length approach whose architect was Herbert Morrison. The essence of this model is that ministers are responsible for policy but the boards of the industries are to be free from political interference on day-to-day matters of management. This blueprint was enshrined in the nationalisation Acts by reserving to ministers powers to appoint and in certain situations dismiss the chairmen and members of the boards in charge of the running of the industries, the power to give general directions on matters affecting the national interest, the need for ministerial approval of certain programmes such as development or reorganisation involving substantial capital expenditure, and the ability to request information at any time. Most importantly from a practical point of view, if an industry could not meet its financial obligation to break even, it was the government who had to provide the money. These provisions were intended to give ministers strategic powers of control but to leave the boards freedom to manage the industry within the framework set by the minister and in particular to fix the prices and wages within the industry. This model did not work according to plan. The nationalised industries were too important to be left alone, particularly in the area of prices and wages. If there was a major strike on the railways or in the mines, negotiations took place with union leaders who at one period were invited to No. 10 Downing Street to talks over beer and sandwiches. If there were elections in the offing, pressure was brought to prevent a price increase in a key industry. Mostly pressure was not exerted through a general direction having legal effect under the statute but by informal discussions between the chairman and the minister which were given the nickname of lunch-table directives. The minister would either have appointed the chairman or be in a position not to reappoint him, the term of office usually being for five years. Where the industry needed money, the minister would be in the most powerful position to twist the chairman's arm. Very few general directions were ever issued and it is doubtful whether they could have been legally given in many of the situations where pressure was brought to bear on specific issues. Labour governments used their powers to make particular industries perform social obligations which were financially uneconomic, *e.g.* build a power station which was not yet needed, to provide employment. Mr Heath's government used the nationalised industries as the spearhead of his incomes policy by making them keep prices down.

This political interference with the running of the industries blurred the responsibility for their management and efficiency and played havoc with their finances. It became accepted that an industry which was asked to perform unprofitable social obligations should be compensated by the government (Cmnd. 3437, 1967), though the means and extent were often the subject of much controversy. In spite of this concession, it was generally recognised that the relationship between ministers and the nationalised industries was unsatisfactory. In 1976 an independent inquiry recommended a new approach (National Economic Development Office). Instead of the arm's length approach which it thought had broken down and which it rejected as inappropriate for industries so vital to the economy of the country, it recommended a new structure based on co-operation between ministers and industries in a new body (the Policy Council) to be inserted between the minister and the boards where mutually agreed policies would be hammered out. Concertation rather than separation between minister and industry was to be the key. The Labour government, significantly, rejected these recommendations as imposing an unnecessary additional layer between the minister and the board (Cmnd. 7131, 1978). It also disputed that there could be a clear-cut distinction between strategic decisions to be taken by the Policy Council and managerial decisions to be taken by the board of the industry, but it eagerly embraced the committee's recommendation to give ministers a last-resort power to give specific and not just general directions, which it promised to use sparingly. This promise never had to be implemented because Mrs Thatcher's government which followed had a very different philosophy towards the nationalised industries.

In theory the Conservative government espoused a hands-off approach. The nationalised industries were to be treated like private industry and the aim was that they should all as soon as possible pay their way and not rely on government subsidies. This did not prevent governmental interference during the miners' strike of 1984–85 in spite of the government's declared policy of neutrality. The overriding constraint imposed by the government was the financial limit within which each industry had to work. These limits determined how much an industry could borrow, or, if it was profitable like the gas and electricity industries or the Post Office, how much money it had to pay back to the government. These limits were fixed with reference to the government's monetary policy and they in turn determined the prices which the industry had to charge. Thus the government's economic policy determined the prices which the consumer had to pay rather than the financial state of the industry. Non-interference by the government was therefore practised more in theory than reality.

The Conservative governments' main solution to the problems arising from the relationship between the government and the nationalised industries was de-nationalisation. The slogan was that the proper business of government is not the government of business. The Conservatives privatised almost every public utility ranging from British Telecommunications to the Railways and including coal, gas, electricity and water. The only exceptions were the canals, the London Underground and the Post Office. The latter was saved from privatisation under Mr Major's government because a few Conservative M.P.s and the Ulster Unionists feared this would lead to the closure of rural post offices and endanger the uniform postal rate to all parts of the United Kingdom. In other words, due to the government's small majority in Parliament social considerations triumphed over economic ones. The Labour government which was elected in 1997 has tried to reconcile them by turning the Post Office into a wholly government-owned public limited company (plc) to emphasise its commercial independence. It will have more commercial freedom and less financial constraints, though the

Treasury will still set the dividend which the Post Office will have to pay to the government and control the amount that can be borrowed over a certain figure. The Post Office's obligation to supply a universal service at a uniform rate is now enshrined in law and will be policed by a regulator but the problem of rural post offices and the whole post office network has by no means been solved.

Here commercial considerations cannot be reconciled with social obligations. There has been a steady decline in the number of post offices in rural areas and deprived urban areas and there would be a sharp decline in business when social security payments are automatically transferred to the bank accounts of recipients. If market forces were allowed to operate, a vital social resource would have to close down. The government has, therefore, been pressured into providing alternative sources of revenue such as banking facilities, internet access and provision of advice and information on government services. A duty has been placed on the Post Office to maintain the rural network and prevent any avoidable closures. There is even provision in the Postal Services Act 2000 (section 103) to provide a government subsidy to post offices. Plus ça change plus c'est la même chose. This provision harks back to the 1960s and 1970s. It illustrates that there are limits to the delegation of political power to independent bodies. When the issue is politically sensitive and pressures are sufficiently strong, the government cannot opt out but is forced to intervene and will be politically accountable for its interference.

However, privatisation has not eliminated the problem of governmental interference. The government may retain a stake in some industries. Even where all the shares have been sold, the government may retain a special share to use in case of a foreign takeover or other emergency. Governments declared that they will treat these companies in the same way as a private sector company and will not use any shareholding they retain to interfere in the commercial decisions of the company except in the circumstances envisaged for the use of the special share. They do, however, retain the power to use their shareholding where this exists and a subsequent government would *a fortiori* not be bound by such a declaration.

The revelation of the pressures brought to bear on British Aerospace, in which the government only retained a special share, to withdraw from the European consortium which made a bid to take over Westland Helicopters, and the arm-twisting to which the fully private firm of Westland itself (as supplier of helicopters to the armed services) was subjected by both camps in the government made a mockery of the policy of non-interference with industry which the government professed. On the other hand in debates over the pit closures the government argued that it could not legally bring pressure on the electricity generating companies in which it held 40 per cent of the shares to make them buy more coal so as to reprieve more pits (H.L. Deb., vol. 539, col. 675, October 20, 1992).

The pit closure issue illustrates that the government cannot opt out of policy decisions of this magnitude. Though it was the still nationalised British Coal's responsibility to close down pits, the government had to face the political fall-out and to pick up the bill for redundancies and the resulting devastation in the mining communities. The pit closure issue also shows that privatisation does not absolve the government from responsibility. It was the way in which the electricity industry was privatised that led to the "dash for gas", *i.e.* the building of gas-fired power stations with the Secretary of State's consent which reduced the demand for coal. This in turn led to interference by the Labour government who imposed a moratorium on new gas-fired power stations pending a review of the wholesale electricity market, itself a legacy of privatisation. The wheel turned full circle when the Labour government agreed to subsidise the privatised coal industry to prevent pit closures (H.C. Deb. vol. 348, col. 697, April 17, 2000), reviving memories of nationalisation.

The regulators, who have been appointed to oversee each privatised utility, are charged with protecting the interests of consumers, promoting competition, regulating prices and ensuring efficiency. They are the new guardians of the public interest and they raise in a new form the same conflict between independence and accountability which bedevilled the nationalised industries. One far-seeing commentator on these new quangos asked: "Is this going to be a way of privatising what are on occasion political judgments?" (Walker, 1990, p. 157). Nowhere is this better illustrated than in the Labour government's decision to entrust the Post Office regulator with reviewing the Post Office's monopoly for delivering letters costing less than £1, and revoke its earlier decision to reduce the monopoly (Postal Services Act 2000, section 8 and H.C. Deb. vol. 340, col. 939, December 8, 1999).

The most significant example of shedding political power was the announcement a few days after the 1997 General Election by the Chancellor of the Exchequer that the setting of interest rates would be the responsibility of the Bank of England with immediate effect. However, the Chancellor lays down the inflation target which the interest rate is set to achieve. The government also appoints directly seven of the nine members of the Monetary Policy Committee of the Bank who decide the level of interest rates each month and the other two members are appointed by the Governor of the Bank, who is himself appointed by the government. There is, too, a reserve power for the Treasury to override the Bank temporarily in extreme economic circumstances by an order subject to Parliamentary approval (Bank of England Act 1998, Part II).

This fundamental change implemented a manifesto commitment to free decision-making on monetary policy from "short-term political manipulation" and to make it more open and accountable. The Bank and its Monetary Policy Committee are directly accountable to the Treasury Committee of the House of Commons which holds regular hearings with them and the Chancellor on monetary policy. The House of Lords also has a Select Committee on the Monetary Policy Committee of the Bank. But the House of Commons Treasury Committee was unable to persuade the government to give it a statutory role in confirming appointments to the Monetary Policy Committee. This has not prevented the Treasury Committee from holding non-statutory hearings into the professional competence and personal independence of candidates (H.C. 822 (1997–98)). Minutes of the meeting of the Monetary Policy Committee of the Bank have to be published within six weeks and are in fact published two weeks later.

These changes to one of the most important powers over the economy were received with almost universal acclaim. But there were dissenting voices particularly among Labour M.P.s, who saw it as a vote of no confidence in political decision-making. As one of them said, "there are serious implications for democracy" (H.C. Deb. vol. 295, col. 1060, June 11, 1997).

Local authorities

The relationship between the central government and local authorities is again a different one. Local authorities are the only public bodies apart from the House of Commons and now the devolved legislatures which are directly elected. Local councillors, therefore, represent and are accountable to their local electorate which gives them a legitimacy quite different from that of an appointed body and which can lead to direct conflict with central government, particularly one of a different political persuasion. However, in our constitution, whose linchpin is the sovereignty of Parliament, the central government with a majority in the House of Commons has the last word through being able to pass legislation. The increase in recent years of legislation to regulate the relationship between central and local government is indicative of its breakdown, as traditionally this has been based on consensus, consultation and co-operation rather than law.

Local authorities derive all their powers from Acts of Parliament in which the government of the day lays down its policy in respect of a particular subject-matter whether it be housing, education or town and country planning and delimits the functions which local authorities perform in that field. Local authorities in this country have no general powers to carry on activities outside their statutory powers though there is now a broad new power to promote or improve the economic, social or environmental well-being of their area or their inhabitants (Local Government Act 2000, Part I). The Conservative governments between 1979 and 1997 legislated on an unprecedented scale passing over 60 Acts of Parliament relating to local government. There were three strands running through this legislation, namely centralisation, privatisation and structural reorganisation. Centralisation takes various forms, such as provisions for ministerial guidance to which local authorities have to have regard, providing rights of appeal to ministers from local decisions, *e.g.* refusal of planning permission, powers of inspection and reserve powers to act where the local authority has failed to perform one of its functions. It was the increasing use of prescriptive legal provisions instead of persuasion through advice and non-statutory guidance which marked the breakdown of consensus between local and central government, and nowhere was this more marked than in the case of local government finance whose control enables central government to wield most power over local authorities and which has given rise to the greatest conflict.

Local authorities derive their finance from locally raised revenue, central government grants, charges and fees, and in the case of capital expenditure mainly from loans and capital receipts. The main conflict between central and local government in recent years has arisen over the attempt, particularly by Mrs Thatcher's government, to control local government expenditure in furtherance of the government's economic policies. The previous Labour government had tried to curb local authorities' current expenditure by imposing strict limits to prevent the central government grant increasing in line with local expenditure and by reducing the total grant available to all authorities if they collectively overshot the totals of expenditure indicated by central government. The Conservative government changed the law in the Local Government, Planning and Land Act 1980 so as to enable the grant allocated to individual authorities to be tailored to reflect the extent to which they complied with the figure which the central government department determined to be the correct expenditure for each authority, so that increases in expenditure above a certain level attracted less grant. Even though this figure was not legally binding, it represented an inroad on the autonomy of local authorities to determine their own expenditure. Control was further tightened in 1982. When these measures did not have the desired effect because local authorities could make good the shortfall of income from government grant by levying higher rates to finance their expenditure, the government in the Rates Act 1984 took powers to impose rate-capping on local authorities which allowed the minister to fix the maximum rates of those authorities who spent above another set of limits laid down by the minister. Thus power of a local authority to fix its own rates was for the first time interfered with by central government. The rates as such came under attack next. Mrs Thatcher had given a pledge to abolish the rates when she was Leader of the Opposition and when the revaluation of properties on which rates were levied caused an outcry in Scotland, the pledge was honoured and Scotland became the guinea pig for the hated community charge which contributed so much to Mrs Thatcher's downfall. Its rationale and hence its nickname poll tax was that everyone, however poor, should pay something towards local government expenditure, unlike rates, which were levied only on occupiers of property. The rhetoric for the poll tax stressed accountability and fairness, namely that all those who could vote for local expenditure should have to pay towards it and that a person living alone should not have to pay the same as the household of several adults living next door. The reality was the gross unfairness of a flat-rate charge which was unrelated to income and the 20 per cent charge on students and those on income support which led to poll tax riots and enormous enforcement problems with millions of summonses to non-payers, many of whom disenfranchised themselves by removing themselves from the electoral register to avoid detection, with profound consequences for democracy.

The poll tax was introduced in April 1990; Mrs Thatcher was deposed in November 1990 and in the 1991 Budget VAT was increased to 17½ per cent to pay for a poll tax rebate of £140 per head. The Bill providing for the new council tax to replace the poll tax was rushed through the House of Commons after its introduction in November 1991. The tax tried to avoid the pitfalls of the poll tax without jettisoning it completely. It, therefore, returned to a property-based tax but retained a personal element in the form of a discount for single person households. The tax is levied on domestic properties which are divided into eight bands according to their capital value so that those in the highest band pay three times as much tax as those in the lowest band. This removed the unfairness of the flat-rate poll tax to some extent, though the differential between the top and the bottom band was skewed in favour of the better off. The tax was based on a two person household thus deliberately not charging large households more tax unlike the poll tax. There was also abandonment of the principle that all voters must pay something by abolishing the 20 per cent levy on students and those on income support. The main survivor from the poll tax principle was the discount for single person households. The Labour government has retained the council tax intact.

There was no change under the council tax to the amount of local government expenditure to be funded from the tax in relation to other sources of revenue, such as the rate levied on business property which is fixed by the government and the grant paid by central government. This is assessed on the basis of what the government thinks each local authority should spend, the issue which began the assault on local government expenditure in 1980. Since the council tax now funds only about one-quarter of local government expenditure it has to rise very steeply for every pound of expenditure over the amount calculated as necessary by the government. The Labour government has modified the provision for capping council tax rises by allowing targeting of individual authorities instead of setting a limit to which all authorities were expected to conform (Local Government Act 1999, Part II). It intends to use the power very sparingly — a small step away from centralisation.

There was an even more fundamental assault on local government than the financial stranglehold by central government. The Conservative government was intent on transforming local authorities from being providers of services to enabling others to provide them and saw the role of local authorities as setting standards and monitoring performance (Consultation Paper: *The Structure of Local Government in England*, 1991). This revolution was accomplished through privatisation in various forms of local authority services.

The selling of council houses, the opting-out of schools which became grant-maintained and the contracting out of services through competitive tendering were all aspects of this development. Again modifications were made by the Labour government. In particular compulsory competitive tendering was replaced by a new system for promoting efficiency through national performance indicators and performance reviews which is called "Best Value" (Local Government Act 1999, Part I). There were also important changes in the organisation of schools but the Labour government has not reversed the fundamental transformation of the role of local authorities started by the Conservatives.

This transformation of the functions of local government was used to support the case for the reorganisation of the structure of local government less than 20 years after the last major upheaval of local authorities in 1974. Because of the changing role of local authorities the Conservative government argued that there is now no ideal size which an authority must have to deliver services (Consultation Paper, 1991 (*supra*) para. 21). There was also no need for a uniform structure, though the government clearly favoured single tier, *i.e.* unitary authorities, which was the existing structure in London and the metropolitan areas outside London after the abolition of the Greater London Council and the Metropolitan County Councils in 1985 (*ibid.*, para. 25 *et seq*). A Local Government Commission for England was set up to review the structure of local authorities in England area by area in accordance with guidance from the Secretary of State for the Environment. The result was not what had been anticipated. Unlike the position in Scotland and Wales, where unitary authorities were imposed on both countries by Acts of Parliament in 1994 (Local Government (Scotland) and Local Government (Wales) Acts), no uniform pattern for England outside London and the metropolitan areas emerged. After an elaborate consultation exercise the Commission found little enthusiasm for change from the existing two-tier structure in many parts of the country. In most of England the two-tier structure of county councils as the top tier and district councils as the lower tier remained intact. The new unitary authorities which were created were mainly big cities or resulted from dismembering county councils which were newly created in 1974. These changes were largely uncontroversial across the political spectrum and were, therefore, left untouched by the Labour government which concentrated on restructuring the government of London and on "modernising" the decision-making process of local authorities.

After holding a referendum in London in May 1998 (at which the turnout was 34 per cent) the Labour government set up the Greater London Authority consisting of a directly elected Mayor and an elected Assembly of 25 members (see Chapter I). The new authority bears little resemblance to the Greater London Council (GLC) which was abolished in 1985, either in composition or functions. It is intended to restore a voice for London but it is squeezed between the central government on the one hand and London borough councils on the other. London borough councils are unitary authorities performing all the functions of a local authority. The Greater London Authority (GLA), unlike the old GLC, is not the top tier of a two-tier system of local government in which the functions are divided between the two tiers of local authorities. The functions it has been allocated are mainly those which were entrusted to quangos after the abolition of the GLC, namely Transport, Police, Fire & Emergency Planning and Economic Development, for which a new quango was created by the Regional Development Agencies Act 1998. These quangos are now made accountable to the GLA and the Mayor either appoints or nominates the members who, in the case of the Metropolitan Police Authority and the Fire Authority, comprise a majority of Assembly members. The Mayor either has to produce or approve strategies for transport, economic development, land use planning, the environment and culture. These will be implemented by the quangos or other bodies. When drawing up the strategies the Mayor has to consult the Assembly but its only real power is over the budget, which is drawn up by the Mayor, but can be amended by the Assembly by a two-thirds majority. The Greater London Authority and the functional bodies (quangos) for which it is responsible are financed in the same way as other local authorities but the Mayor has a new controversial power to introduce charges on road use and workplace parking (Greater London Authority Act 1999, ss. 295 and 296).

The Mayor is not a member of the Assembly but must appoint a Deputy from the members of the Assembly. The Mayor is accountable to the Assembly by being required to make monthly reports and attend meetings of the Assembly ten times a year to answer questions and he has to make an annual report and hold an annual "State of London" debate. The lines of accountability between the Mayor and the Assembly have been somewhat blurred by the first elected Mayor, Ken Livingstone, who has taken several Assembly members into his advisory cabinet. The separation of powers between the directly elected Mayor and the elected Assembly to whom he is accountable represents a completely new method of decision-making in local government. London has blazed the trail for the rest of the country where the decision-making structure is being remodelled under the Local Government Act 2000.

The justification given for this fundamental change is efficiency. The existing procedure under which decisions are mainly made by local councillors in committees is criticised as time-wasting. The committees have to be in proportion to the party political balance on the council (Local Government and Housing Act 1989, s. 15) and, therefore, where one party has an overall majority, the result may be a foregone conclusion, as party groups will have met beforehand to decide the policy and the whipping system will almost invariably ensure that this is rubber-stamped. To abolish whipping would not be politically feasible. The government's remedy was to model local government decision-making on that of central government by separating the executive, that is the decision-making function, from the scrutiny function. This is achieved by forcing councils to adopt one of the three models of executives set out in the Local Government Act 2000 (section 11), apart from the smallest district councils for which the Secretary of State specified alternative arrangements (section 32). The three options are firstly, a directly elected mayor who chooses a cabinet of up to 10 councillors, or secondly, an executive leader elected by the council with a cabinet chosen either by him or the council or thirdly, a directly elected mayor with a local government officer appointed by the council as council manager. An executive which includes an elected mayor has to be approved in a referendum of the voters. The executive, unlike the committees of the council, can consist entirely of members of the majority party. It will exercise all the functions of a local authority except those specifically excluded by the Secretary of State. Licensing functions and the granting of planning permissions are excluded. The budget also requires the approval of the full council. The majority of councillors, who will not be members of the executive, will sit on overview and scrutiny committees (from which members of the executive are excluded), which can call members of the executive before them for questioning and make reports and recommendations but which will have no decision-making powers.

The rationale for this revolutionary change in decision-making is not only efficiency but greater openness. Decisions will no longer be made in the party caucus behind closed doors but they may now be made by the one-party executive behind similarly closed doors. It is for the executive to decide whether to meet in private or public, except where the Secretary of State specifies in regulations that meetings must be either open to the public or private (section 22). The regulations provide that meetings of the executive must be held in public where the person presiding reasonably believes that a key decision will be made at the meeting. Key decisions are defined as those likely to result in significant expenditure or to have significant effect on local communities. The room for discretion in applying these provisions is obviously considerable, though this is delimited by guidance and a scrutiny committee can demand an explanation. When a key decision is to be made by an individual rather than a committee, a report which he intends to take into consideration must be made public and supplied to the relevant scrutiny committee.

The old council committees did not necessarily rubber-stamp party decisions especially where no party had a majority and the Parliamentary committee, which scrutinised the Local Government Bill before it was introduced in Parliament, found that the old committee system had a role to play in educating councillors (H.C. 542 (1998–99) para. 144). The driving force behind these reforms is efficiency rather than democracy, as in other areas of modernisation. The Local Government Act 2000 is itself an example of a skeleton Act (see Chapter 2), as it leaves so many matters to be prescribed by the Secretary of State and consequently further centralises power away from local authorities, as well as centralising power within local authorities by concentrating it within the executive.

The missing link in the reforms of local government in England, outside London, is a tier of elected regional government which would have a strategic and co-ordinating role analogous to that of the Greater London Authority. Such a tier would sit uneasily on top of the two-tier structure of local authorities in most of the English counties. A regional tier is developing through some decentralisation by central government. Nine regional development agencies have been created (including the one in London) which have strategic functions such as drawing up regional economic strategies (Regional Development Agencies Act 1998). They are being overseen by non-statutory regional assemblies consisting of councillors, business people, trade unionists and others. Whether this heralds the beginning of devolution to the English regions will be considered after examining devolution to Scotland and Wales.

DEVOLUTION

In September 1997 referendums were held in Scotland and Wales on devolution after the publication of White Papers setting out the proposals but before legislation had been drafted. This was a deliberate departure from the previous attempt at devolution in 1979 where the legislation preceded the referendums which were unsuccessful. In Scotland three-quarters of the voters were in favour of a Scottish Parliament on a turnout of 60 per cent, whereas in Wales the majority in favour of a Welsh Assembly was 0.6 per cent on a turnout of 50 per cent. The Scotland Act and the Government of Wales Act became law in 1998 and the elections were held in May 1999.

Devolution is a generic term which covers a number of different schemes, as is illustrated by the distinction between devolution to Scotland and Wales, but there is a common denominator between them. Devolution is distinguished from federalism by sovereignty remaining undivided in the U.K. Parliament; it is distinguishable from decentralisation by the creation of elected bodies, which may have widely differing powers.

The Scottish Parliament and the Welsh Assembly have very different functions. The Scottish Parliament has power to pass Acts except on matters which are reserved for the U.K. Parliament, which are listed in the Scotland Act 1998 (Schedule 5). They include foreign affairs (including the European Union), defence, the civil service, the Crown and Parliament of the U.K., economic and monetary policy, social security and abortion. In contrast the Welsh Assembly cannot pass Acts but exercises the functions of the Secretary of State for Wales which have been transferred to it including the power to make subordinate legislation (Government of Wales Act 1998, Part II). The Assembly has the Welsh Health Authorities and Welsh quangos within its remit.

The working of these devolved legislatures is very different from that of the U.K. Parliament. Firstly, they are elected for a fixed term which is four years. In the case of the Scottish Parliament there is provision for an extraordinary General Election if two-thirds of the members of Parliament (*i.e.* 86 members) vote that the Parliament be dissolved or if the Parliament fails to nominate a First Minister within 28 days (Scotland Act, s. 3). This could arise as the system of proportional representation (see Chapter 1) may not and did not produce an overall majority of seats for one party. In Scotland Labour won the largest number of seats (56) but far short of an absolute majority. They were able to form a coalition with the Liberal Democrats who came in fourth place behind the Conservatives. In Wales Labour won 28 out of 60 seats and chose to form a minority administration but formed a coalition with the Liberal Democrats in October, 2000. The nationalist parties in each case were the largest opposition party. In both Scotland and Wales the relationship between the executive and the legislature is modelled on that of the U.K. Parliament. The Scotland Act 1998 (Part II) provides for Parliament to nominate one of its members for appointment by the Queen as First Minister, who appoints Ministers from the members with the agreement of Parliament. The First Minister must resign if Parliament passes a vote of no confidence which will not, however, trigger a General Election unless two-thirds of members so wish or negotiations to nominate a new First Minister are unsuccessful.

In Wales, it was only during the Government of Wales Bill's passage through Parliament that the government put down amendments for setting up an Executive Committee consisting of the First Secretary (now referred to as First Minister) elected by the Assembly and Assembly Secretaries appointed by him from among the Assembly members (Government of Wales Act 1998, Part III). These amendments were introduced to enable the Assembly to operate a Cabinet-style process of decision-making by the delegation of functions to the Executive Committee and the First Secretary instead of the Committee model of decision-making of the old style local government. The model was tested in February 2000 when a no confidence motion in the First Secretary was tabled by the opposition which led to his resignation. His successor, who was elected by the party as Labour leader, was not opposed for nomination as First Secretary. However, when a few months earlier a censure motion was passed in the Assembly on the agriculture secretary, she did not resign and she was supported by the then First Secretary. At Westminster such a motion would be treated as a vote of no confidence in the government (see Chapter I). It is clear that different conventions must evolve in a fixed-term legislature, where there is no provision for early dissolution.

The most important difference between the U.K. Parliament and the devolved legislatures lies in the committee structure. In Scotland there are 16 committees in total including eight subject committees which shadow the departments in the executive. The membership has to be proportionate to the political balance in the Parliament and the chair is not necessarily from a governing party. The committees, unlike the departmental committees in Westminster, have the functions of scrutinising and even initiating legislation as well as conducting inquiries by questioning Ministers, civil servants and outside bodies. There is also an all-party Parliamentary Bureau (consisting of the business managers of the four main parties) and a Presiding Officer who is elected by secret ballot by the Parliament. The Parliamentary Bureau carries out the functions performed by the government through the "usual channels", namely the Whips' offices, in Westminster. These procedures are intended to facilitate a more consensual, participative and less adversarial type of politics appropriate for power-sharing between parties, which is the outcome of a proportional voting system. The reality may not match the intention for, as has been said, "a new Parliament does not guarantee new politics". (Brown, 2000, p. 554). However, at least one Bill, abolishing warrant sales, was passed against the wishes of the Executive.

The Welsh Assembly is structured on similar lines with six Committees, which have to be politically balanced, shadowing departments. But here the Assembly Secretary (now referred to as Minister), who is a member of the Executive, is also a member of the committee, whilst the chair may belong to an Opposition party. This reflects the dual functions of the committees who both develop policy and scrutinise it. This could lead to conflict between the Assembly Secretary and the committee but, where the Secretary is exercising functions delegated to him, his decision will prevail. The committees also deal with delegated legislation which has to be approved by the Assembly. There is, too, an all-party Business Committee which advises the Business Manager, equivalent to the government Chief Whip, on the arrangement of business of the Assembly. The Assembly committees sit in public but not the Executive Committee, though the new First Minister publishes its minutes on the Assembly's website, six weeks in arrears.

Devolution affects not only the countries to whom power has been devolved, it has repercussions on the whole United Kingdom. Some of the issues have been addressed in the arrangements for devolution, others have been left unresolved and could be time-bombs waiting to explode and lead to the break-up of the United Kingdom.

One of the unifying factors contained in the devolution arrangements is the civil service. Scottish and Welsh civil servants will remain part of the Home Civil Service but they "will work through the First Minister" in Scotland (or First Secretary in Wales) to the Crown (H.C. Deb., vol. 319, col. 439, November 11, 1998).

Another unifying factor consists of the Concordats or series of agreements between the U.K. government and the devolved administrations in Scotland and Wales setting out the principles which will underlie relations between them. They are not legally binding (Cm 4444, 1999). The principal agreement set up a Joint Ministerial Committee consisting of U.K. Ministers and their equivalents from the devolved administrations (including Northern Ireland). It will consider devolved and non-devolved matters which impinge on each other and consider disputes between the administrations. It can also resolve differences between the U.K. and one of the devolved administrations, when it will consist of the appropriate Ministers from the U.K. and the respective administration. When university tuition fees were abolished for Scottish students in Scotland no meeting of the Joint Ministerial Committee was called, as there was perceived to be no problem that could not be resolved by normal communications between the two administrations (H.L. Deb., vol. 609, col. 227, February 2, 2000). Nevertheless, this could be one of the time-bombs ticking away, particularly as it involves public expenditure.

The financing of the devolved administrations has not so far caused serious controversy but this may blow up in the future. Scotland and Wales are financed by block-grants which are voted by the U.K. Parliament. They are spent in accordance with budgets approved by the devolved legislatures. The Scottish Parliament also has a power to increase or reduce income-tax by 3p, which has not yet been used (Scotland Act 1998, Part IV). The formula used for fixing the block-grant, known as the Barnett formula, is a way of sharing out changes in public expenditure on a population basis, but this does not determine the total level of the grant, which also includes an inherited element which embodies higher public expenditure per head in Scotland and Wales than in England (H.C. 341 (1997–98)). It is this discrepancy which carries the seeds of future discord, especially as income per head in some of the English regions is now below that in Scotland, though not below that in Wales.

The courts are another unifying element, in particular the Judicial Committee of the Privy Council (consisting substantially of the Law Lords), to whom a Bill of the Scottish Parliament can be referred to determine whether it falls within the competence of the Scottish Parliament before it becomes law. The Bill must not

be presented for the Royal Assent where the Court finds it is outside the Parliament's powers (Scotland Act 1998, ss. 32 and 33).
Courts in all parts of the United Kingdom are also competent to
rule on the competence of a Scottish Act after it has been passed
(Schedule 6). Subordinate legislation of the Welsh Assembly is
subject to judicial review in the normal way (see below) and such
cases may now be heard in Wales instead of London (Practice
Direction (Supreme Court: Devolution), [1999] 1 W.L.R. 1592).

The most important symbol of the unity of the United Kingdom
is, of course, the U.K. Parliament, but it also harbours within it the
most politically explosive issue, the West Lothian question (see
below). The sovereignty of the U.K. Parliament is specifically
enshrined in the Scotland Act (section 28(7)); however, the principal agreement or Concordat states, "the U.K. Government will
proceed in accordance with the convention that the U.K. Parliament would not normally legislate with regard to devolved matters except with the agreement of the devolved legislature" (Cm
4444, para. 13). This convention was put into operation when the
Scottish Parliament consented to the U.K. Parliament legislating to
lower the age of consent for homosexual acts in the Sexual
Offences (Amendment) Bill (see above, Chapter 2).

Devolution has affected Parliamentary questions which U.K.
Ministers can be asked by M.P.s. They will not be able to table
questions relating to devolved matters, except where such matters are included in U.K. legislation or concerned with the concordats or where U.K. Ministers retain administrative powers or
can require information from the devolved executive (H.C. Deb.,
vol. 336, col. 761, October 25, 1999). The Parliamentary committees on Scottish and Welsh Affairs have had their terms of reference amended to reflect the consequences of devolution.

No changes have so far been made in relation to the legislative process, where the West Lothian question becomes relevant.
It is named after Mr Tam Dalyell, who was M.P. for West Lothian when he first posed the problem, which is that Scottish M.P.s
will be able to vote in the U.K. Parliament on legislation which
does not extend to Scotland, whereas English M.P.s will not be
able to influence Scottish legislation. It raises the spectre of a
U.K. government with a small majority being able to pass legislation on English matters only with the help of Scottish M.P.s, as
would have been the case when Labour was in power from
1964–66 and in 1974. It is, of course, precisely what happened in
reverse to Scotland during 18 years of Conservative government, which increased the pressure for devolution. The only

provision in the Scotland Act 1998 which has some relevance to the issue is the provision (section 86) which removes the higher quota of M.P.s that Scotland has hitherto enjoyed, but this will not take effect until the Parliamentary constituency boundaries are redrawn. This will not, however, solve the West Lothian question. In contrast the Scotland Act 1978, which never came into force, provided that, where a Bill not relating to Scotland was passed by the vote of Scottish M.P.s, there had to be a second vote confirming that the Bill should be read a second time (section 66).

There have been a number of suggested solutions to the West Lothian question. Some are based on a self-denying ordinance, or a Standing Order of the House of Commons, preventing Scottish M.P.s from voting on English or Welsh matters. This does, however, involve having M.P.s with unequal status and, more importantly, might make it impossible for a government to get its legislation passed (H.C. 460 (1997–98) para. 53), which could be the reason that it has not found favour with the government but has been supported by the Leader of the Opposition.

Other suggestions would adapt the legislative process for Bills dealing exclusively with one of the countries of the United Kingdom. The Procedure Committee of the House of Commons has recommended that the Speaker should be able to certify that a Bill related exclusively to one of the constituent parts of the United Kingdom and that the Second Reading (the first debate on the Bill) should take place in a committee with a minimum number of M.P.s from that part of the U.K. and that detailed consideration of the Bill should take place in a Standing Committee with a core of M.P.s from that part. These recommendations would require the rule that committees must be constituted in proportion to the political balance in the House of Commons to be relaxed (H.C. 185 (1998–99) para. 23 *et seq.*). None of these committees would be able to make decisions which could not be overturned on the floor of the House of Commons, where the West Lothian question would arise once more.

The government did not accept the Procedure Committee's proposals but they did resuscitate the Standing Committee on Regional Affairs which was originally set up in 1975 but has been moribund since 1979. It is to consist of 13 M.P.s representing English constituencies but the political balance must be that of the whole House. A Liberal Democrat amendment to alter this so that the party balance would reflect that of English M.P.s alone was promptly defeated. The committee will not have any teeth. It will only be able to consider matters referred to it by a Minister and the only motion it can pass is that it has considered the matter. It will, however, be able to meet in the English regions and have the power to question a Minister on a statement for up to one and a half hours. Perhaps the fairest verdict on the committee is that half a loaf is better than no bread (H.C. Deb., Vol. 348, col. 289, *et seq.*, April 11, 2000).

We are left with the problem whether there is a satisfactory solution to the West Lothian question or whether it is insoluble. An English Parliament, which would represent 85 per cent of the population of the United Kingdom, is not now supported even by the Conservative opposition. This leaves devolution of powers to elected regional assemblies as the only realistic counterpart to devolution to the legislatures in Scotland, Wales and Northern Ireland. Whether this would assuage or provoke a backlash of English nationalism remains to be seen. The verdict of the Scottish Affairs Committee of the House of Commons was that, "the reform is being conceived piecemeal; if there is an overall blue-print showing how all the pieces will fit together, none of our witnesses were aware of it" (H.C. 460 (1997–98) para. 31). If the fully reformed House of Lords were to be wholly or partly elected on a regional basis this would provide a Parliamentary forum where the regions and countries of the United Kingdom were represented. The Royal Commission on the Reform of the House of Lords saw the Lords as providing, "a voice in Parliament for all the nations and regions of the United Kingdom" (Cm 4534, Chapter 6.20). The strength of the voice would depend on the number of such members. But even a House of Lords wholly elected on regional lines would not solve the West Lothian question, though it might reduce its significance.

5

CONTROL MECHANISMS AND PUBLIC ACCOUNTABILITY

There are a number of mechanisms whereby those who exercise the functions discussed in the previous chapter can be supervised, monitored and held to account. The courts, though numerically they deal with only a small number of cases, are perhaps constitutionally the most significant because the subjection of public authorities to the ordinary courts is the cornerstone of the rule of law as formulated by Dicey in his *Law of the Constitution* (1885, Chapter IV).

COURTS

The courts cannot act as courts of appeal from any of the bodies examined in the previous chapter unless there are express statutory provisions to this effect. They do, however, possess the power to review the decisions of such bodies unless there are express statutory provisions excluding judicial control. Judicial review is more limited than appeal as it is not concerned with the merits of the decision but with its propriety, though in practice the distinction may be a fine one.

Judicial review

A claim for judicial review is now defined as a claim to review the lawfulness of an enactment or a decision or a failure to act in relation to the exercise of a public function (Civil Procedure Rules 1998, Part 54). If the claimant is seeking a mandatory, prohibiting or quashing order he must use the judicial review procedure. Where the claimant's private rights are infringed by a public body and he is seeking the private law remedies of a declaration, injunction or damages, the ordinary procedure for civil actions is still applicable (*O'Reilly v. Mackman*, 1983).

The judicial review procedure has very distinctive features. Claims are dealt with in the Administrative Court by judges specialising in administrative law. Permission has to be obtained from the court to proceed with a claim which will usually be determined in the first instance without an oral hearing. The claim has to be made within a strict time-limit of three months. The claimant must state the grounds for bringing judicial review proceedings and name anyone he considers to be directly affected by the claim. He must have a sufficient interest in bringing the proceedings. This includes not only those adversely affected but has been increasingly extended to pressure groups acting in the public interest, as is illustrated by the World Development Movement being allowed to challenge the legality of financial aid for the Pergau dam (*R. v. Secretary of State for Foreign Affairs ex parte World Development Movement Ltd*, 1995, see below). The court also has power to hear any person who wishes to make representations. Evidence is presented in the form of written affidavits rather than orally through witnesses, a procedure which is not suitable for resolving disputed questions of fact, which will not normally be an issue in such proceedings. Cases may be transferred to or from the Administrative Court if they have been started in the wrong forum.

The grounds on which judicial review may be allowed have been categorised by Lord Diplock in his judgement in *Council of Civil Service Unions v. Minister for the Civil Service* (1984: *GCHQ* case) where judicial review was requested of the Prime Minister's instruction prohibiting staff employed in the Government Communications Headquarters to be members of a trade union. He classified the grounds for judicial review under three headings, namely, illegality, irrationality and procedural impropriety. The case decides that the same grounds of review are available whether the powers are derived from statute or from the residual common law powers of the Crown (the prerogative), as in the case itself, though they may not be applicable to such prerogative powers as the dissolution of Parliament or the granting of honours. However, in *R. v. Secretary of State for the Home Department ex parte Bentley* (1994), it was held that even the royal prerogative of mercy, *i.e.* to grant a pardon to someone who has been convicted, is reviewable by the courts.

Illegality. Under the heading of illegality Lord Diplock said, "the decision-maker must understand correctly the law that regulates his decision-making power and must give effect to it" (*GCHQ*, p. 1196). The difficulty is to distinguish a mistake of law that regulates the decision-making power (error going to jurisdiction) from a mistake of law which the decision-maker has the authority to determine (error of law). The distinction between the law which delimits the jurisdiction of the decision-maker and that which is within his jurisdiction was for practical purposes eliminated in the *Anisminic* case (1969) when a decision of the Foreign Compensation Commission, a body set up to distribute compensation for property expropriated abroad, was declared invalid for misconstruction of provisions it was supposed to interpret, although the decisions were expressly declared in the statute as not being open to challenge in any court. By holding that the decision of the Commission was void, the House of Lords set aside the exclusion clause. As a result of the decision any error of law of a decision-making body is open to judicial review. Taken to its logical conclusion this would enable the courts on an application for judicial review to sit in judgment on the interpretation of all the statutory provisions and those contained in delegated legislation which has been entrusted to the various types of decision-making bodies. In practice the courts have not used their powers to the full extent. They may categorise the error as one of fact rather than law where the words to be interpreted are ordinary, non-technical English words, and may leave their interpretation to be determined by the inferior body unless the interpretation is so unreasonable that no reasonable body could reach it, when it would fall within Lord Diplock's second ground of irrationality. The courts will also adopt this approach where they feel the question of interpretation is more suitable for an expert body, which has been set up by Parliament for this purpose, than for the courts. It is, however, very difficult to predict when the courts will adopt the hands-off approach and when they will reinterpret the relevant provisions themselves. This is where extra-legal considerations come into play and the attitude of the judiciary towards questions of social policy may be the hidden premise on which the decision is based.

The attitude of the courts towards issues of policy may be quite explicit when they lay down criteria which the decision-maker must take into account but which are not mentioned in the statutory provisions and may directly contradict statutory provisions which give wide discretionary powers to a body to act as it thinks fit. These limitations which the courts superimpose on statutory provisions may be explicitly designed to protect individual rights, *e.g.* not to be deprived of access to the courts. Thus the courts will, as we saw in the *Anisminic* case, construe any statutory provision to this effect as narrowly as possible, though even here the attitude is not consistent and they have held to be judge-proof clauses which exclude judicial control after six weeks, *e.g.* in the case of compulsory purchase orders, where a reopening of the decision would cause administrative chaos (*R. v. Secretary of State for the Environment ex parte Ostler*, 1977). The courts will also narrowly construe a power to levy a charge from the citizen so that express provision is necessary and even wide discretionary powers will not be sufficient authorisation. Thus a wide power to control food supplies under regulations made to secure the public safety and the defence of the realm did not include a power to charge for the issue of a licence to purchase milk (*AG v. Wiltshire United Dairies*, 1921), and a power to revoke a television licence by a notice in writing did not give the Home Secretary power to revoke a licence which had been renewed before the expiry of the old one so as to avoid paying the increased fee (*Congreve v. Home Office*, 1976).

Similarly the courts have construed legislation and wide discretionary powers exercised under it so as not to take away property rights. The attitude of the judiciary towards great issues of social policy such as slum clearance, council housing and town and country planning can be plotted according to how they have interpreted the legislation *vis-à-vis* the property owner. This has fluctuated from periods of intense hostility to the Housing Acts in the 1930s to a period of acquiescence in town and country planning legislation after 1945 until a reaction set in in the late 1950s when the courts reasserted private property rights in a spate of decisions which emasculated the Town and Country Planning Acts. Parliament engaged in a running battle with the courts at these times, amending the statutes so as to prevent the courts from misinterpreting the legislation, but the courts have the last word on interpretation. The courts can thus limit the ambit of social legislation by superimposing their policy conceptions based on individual rights when interpreting a statute.

Perhaps the most striking illustration of the courts reading limitations into statutory provisions so as to narrow the discretionary powers conferred under them is the duty the courts impose on local authorities to hold the balance between their local taxpayers and other sections of the community. This was one of the grounds on which the GLC's Fares Fair policy, which cut London Transport's fares, was declared unlawful by the courts in *Bromley London Borough Council v. GLC* (1982). Similarly in 1925 in *Roberts v. Hopwood* it was held on the same principle unlawful for a local authority to exercise its powers to pay such wages as it thought fit by paying all its workers male and female a minimum of £4 a week, which was excessive by commercial standards at that time. In contrast the courts held in 1983 in *Pickwell v. Camden London Borough Council* that Camden Borough Council had not acted unlawfully when it settled a strike of manual workers by agreeing a figure above that at which a national settlement was later negotiated. The court said that it was not the basic legal principle which had changed but our attitudes. The real issue is whether the attitude of the courts should prevail over that of the elected local authority in exercising a discretionary power. In the *Camden* case, unlike the *GLC* case and *Roberts v. Hopwood*, the court bent over backwards not to interfere with the judgement of the elected body.

In recent years the courts have been active to an unprecedented extent in reading limitations into statutory provisions. By using this device in a series of causes célèbres in the 1990s, they championed the cause of the most vulnerable members of society and even assumed the role of compensating for the deficiencies of the parliamentary process by making the government legally accountable for the misuse of power.

One of the most striking cases was the Pergau Dam case (*R v. Secretary of State for Foreign Affairs, ex parte World Development Movement Ltd*, 1995). The government had provided financial aid to build a dam in Malaysia which was economically so unsound that the Foreign Secretary had to override the objections of his Permanent Secretary by a direction authorising the expenditure (see below). There were critical Parliamentary reports but it was only the court who could declare the aid to be unlawful. Though the relevant Act gave a blanket power to the Secretary of State to give assistance for promoting the development of a country, the court read in the word "sound" before development. They justified this by the rather tendentious argument that, "if Parliament had intended to confer a power to disburse money for unsound developmental purposes, it could have been expected to say so expressly" (p. 402).

The same technique was employed for the benefit of the poorest citizens in judicial review proceedings against the Lord Chancellor (*R v. Lord Chancellor, ex parte Witham*, 1998). The court declared unlawful an order made by the Lord Chancellor which imposed a fee for bringing a court action, payable even by those receiving income support. The claimant, who was representing himself in a libel action, challenged this order successfully. Laws J made this ringing declaration, "Access to the courts is a constitutional right; it can only be denied by the government if it persuades Parliament to pass legislation which specifically — in effect by express provision — permits the executive to turn people away from the court doors. This has not been done here" (p. 859).

An even more basic right, the right to life, was vindicated by the same means in one of the landmark cases of judicial review, *R v. Secretary of State for Social Security, ex parte Joint Council for the Welfare of Immigrants* (1997). Here the Court of Appeal invalidated regulations removing social security benefits from asylum seekers unless they claimed asylum immediately on arrival in the U.K. After asserting that, "So basic are the human rights here at issue that it cannot be necessary to resort to the European Convention on Human Rights to take note of their violation" (p. 292), Simon Brown LJ continued, "Parliament cannot have intended a significant number of genuine asylum seekers to be impaled on the horns of so intolerable a dilemma: the need either to abandon their claims to refugee status or alternatively to maintain them as best they can but in a state of utter destitution. Primary legislation alone could in my judgment achieve that sorry state of affairs" (p. 293). Parliament promptly achieved that sorry state of affairs by the Asylum and Immigration Act 1996. Parliament asserted its sovereignty but the courts in these cases exposed the deficiencies of the Parliamentary process in holding the executive to account and safeguarding fundamental rights.

In a seminal case of judicial review the court claimed it was upholding the sovereignty of Parliament against prerogative powers exercised by ministers. The Criminal Injuries Compensation Scheme was not created by an Act of Parliament but was embodied in a White Paper in 1964 and derived its authority from the prerogative. In 1988 it was enacted in the Criminal Justice Act but the Act was to come into force only when the Home Secretary made an order bringing it into operation. When the government decided to change the scheme on grounds of expense, it again resorted to a White Paper rather than legislation. The Fire Brigades Union challenged this by judicial review. The case was appealed to the House of Lords who held by a narrow majority that the Home Secretary had acted unlawfully, because he had deprived himself of the power to bring the 1988 Act into force by using the White Paper to amend the scheme and refusing to implement the Act. Lord Browne-Wilkinson put it succinctly, "It is for Parliament, not the executive, to repeal legislation" (*R v. Secretary of State for the Home Department, ex parte Fire Brigades Union*, 1995, p. 474). As a result of the case Parliament was indeed forced to legislate to amend the scheme.

The dissenting Law Lords thought that the court was usurping the function of Parliament to hold the Home Secretary accountable, whereas the majority found that the Home Secretary had usurped Parliament's function to repeal the 1988 Act and they were upholding the supremacy of Parliament. Whether one agrees with the majority or the dissenters, this case like the previous ones exposes the deficiencies in the democratic process. The disagreement is as to whether the courts or Parliament should make good the deficiency.

In none of these cases did the courts resort to Parliamentary debates to find out the real intention of Parliament. This is now possible as a result of the seminal decision of *Pepper v. Hart* (1992). In this case the House of Lords reversed the rule that the courts cannot look at the record of Parliamentary proceedings in Hansard as an aid to statutory interpretation. It held (with the Lord Chancellor dissenting) that reference to Parliamentary material should be permitted where the statute is ambiguous or obscure or the literal meaning would lead to an absurdity and the statement made in Parliament by the minister or the promoter of a Bill makes it clear what the words were intended to mean. In the case itself all these criteria were satisfied as the very point in issue was dealt with by a minister in Standing Committee. This is unlikely to be the case where the courts read limitations into broad statutory provisions.

Irrationality. Lord Diplock's second ground of judicial review in the *GCHQ* case (1984) is irrationality, which he defines as unreasonableness in accordance with the principles of the *Wednesbury* case (1948), *i.e.* "a decision which is so outrageous in its defiance of logic or of accepted moral standards that no sensible person who had applied his mind to the question to be decided could have arrived at it" (*GCHQ*, p. 1196). This principle was construed very narrowly in the *Camden* case so as not to interfere with the judgement of the local authority. However, in the *Secretary of State for Education v. Tameside Borough Council* (1977) the courts had the unenviable task of having to judge the unreasonableness of the decisions of two elected authorities, the minister and the local authority who were in conflict. The Secretary of State for Education had power to give a direction to a local authority which he was satisfied was acting unreasonably. He gave such a direction to the local authority who, after a local election which the Conservatives won, overturned the decision of their Labour predecessors to adopt comprehensive education and abolish grammar schools.

The minister thought there was insufficient time to implement the new selection process before the beginning of the school year. The court applied the very narrow test of unreasonableness to the local authority's actions which had just been approved by the electorate. On the other hand, they held that the minister had no grounds for finding that the local authority had acted unreasonably and that no reasonable minister could so find. This seems to be applying differing tests of unreasonableness to the minister and the local authority. In contrast to this case the Secretary of State for the Environment was held to be acting reasonably when he used his default powers against Norwich City Council (*R. v. Secretary of State for the Environment ex parte Norwich City Council*, 1982) because of their policy of passive resistance to the sale of council houses. As these cases illustrate, the courts were used increasingly as the forum where the conflict between local and central government was fought out. This escalated in the area of local government finance where in case upon case the courts were asked to interpret the complicated provisions of the successive statutes which tightened the financial noose round local authorities. In one of the most important of these cases which challenged the legality of the whole system of targets under the Local Government Finance Act 1982 (*R. v. Secretary of State for the Environment ex parte Nottinghamshire County Council*, 1986) the House of Lords, reversing the Court of Appeal, upheld the decision of the minister. Lord Scarman, with whom the rest of the court agreed, held that in this case, where the minister's decision had to be approved by the House of Commons, "it is not for the judges to say that the action has such unreasonable consequences that the guidance upon which the action is based and of which the House of Commons had notice was perverse and must be set aside. For that is a question of policy for the minister and the Commons, unless there has been bad faith or misconduct by the minister" (pp. 7–8). Even more pointedly, Lord Templeman said, "Judicial review is not just a move in an interminable chess tournament. Although I do not blame Nottingham or Bradford for instituting these proceedings, I hope that in future local authorities will bite on the bullet and not seek to persuade the courts to absolve them from compliance with the Secretary of State's guidance. If for any particular city or for any group of cities guidance is set too low, having regard to their peculiar needs, then persuasion should be offered not to the judges, who are not qualified to listen, but to the department, the minister, all members of parliament and ultimately to the electorate" (p. 23). This impeccable constitutional advice, however, fell on deaf ears and the challenge to the decision to impose a cap on some local authorities to reduce the level of their poll tax predictably failed (*R. v. Secretary of State for the Environment ex parte Hammersmith and Fulham London Borough Council*, 1990). When ministers refuse to give way, Parliament is whipped and the General Election is years ahead, the courts become the political arena because the political remedies do not work. This makes it very difficult for the judges to remain above the political battle, for even judicial abstention, as in the *Nottingham* case, can be seen as taking sides. In our constitution based on the sovereignty of Parliament it is a sign of breakdown of the political system when the courts are used as a political battle-ground.

Procedural impropriety. Lord Diplock's third ground of judicial review is concerned with challenge to the procedure by which the decision is reached rather than with its substance. In practice this may often be the only line of attack open to an applicant who wants a decision to which he objects set aside, because he cannot challenge the decision on its merits by judicial review. The quashing of the decision may be a pyrrhic victory as a new decision may be taken after following the correct procedure but in many cases the victory will in practice be final.

The procedural impropriety may be the result of not following procedural rules laid down by statute or delegated legislation, though the courts will not construe every minor failure to observe such provisions as grounds for striking down such a decision.

Though most tribunals and public inquiries are regulated by procedural rules, many decisions made by ministers, local authorities and other public bodies are not regulated by statutory procedures. It is in this area that the courts have been most creative in fashioning principles to which those who make decisions affecting individuals must conform. The most famous principles are the rules of natural justice which have been applied to a constantly expanding area of decision-making. Though originally the courts distinguished these rules from the more flexible concept of procedural fairness, they are now often treated as synonymous, their application varying according to the subject-matter of the decision. Out of these rules the courts have now developed a new concept of procedural propriety where a legitimate expectation of the applicant is withdrawn.

There are two rules of natural justice which the courts have formulated, namely that no one may be a judge in his own cause and that a person affected by a decision must be given an opportunity to state his case and one person must not be heard behind the back of the other. These basic moral principles, allegedly derived from the Old Testament, have given rise to a myriad of cases to determine their application in a vast variety of situations.

The first rule of natural justice is a rule against bias in the decision-maker. This rule as it affects judges has received a great deal of legal interpretation as a result of the attempt to extradite General Pinochet when he was on a visit to the U.K. Lord Hoffmann, one of the Law Lords who ruled that Pinochet was not immune from extradition as a former Head of State, was chairman of a charity connected with Amnesty, an organisation which had been allowed to intervene in the case. In an unprecedented ruling by five Law Lords this decision was quashed because of Lord Hoffmann's connection with a party to the case. This decision led to a number of cases where it was argued that the judge was disqualified on grounds of bias. In the course of deciding five test cases, a specially selected Court of Appeal laid down guidelines as to what constitutes bias in a judge (*Locabail(UK) Ltd v. Bayfield Properties Ltd*, 2000). The court distinguished between actual bias, which is very rare, automatic disqualification where the judge has an interest in the outcome of the case (as in the Pinochet case) or disqualification if there was a real danger or possibility of bias. The court then laid down guidelines as to what could and could not constitute a real danger of bias.

The rule against bias caused particular difficulty in relation to decisions of ministers who had to hold a public inquiry into objections against a decision made by themselves, *e.g.* to build a road or designate a new town, and ultimately had to decide whether to confirm their own decision after having heard the objectors. Bias in favour of their own decision was built into the decision-making process and the courts held in the famous case concerning Stevenage New Town, *Franklin v. Minister of Town and Country Planning* (1948), that so long as the minister gave genuine consideration to the objections raised at the inquiry he could be as biased in favour of building a new town at Stevenage as he liked. A minister making a policy decision could not be forced into the straitjacket of a judge. This principle has been held not to contravene the right to a fair hearing embodied in the Human Rights Act 1998 (see below Chapter 6).

Similar problems were encountered in applying the second rule of natural justice to ministerial decisions reached after public inquiries. In another landmark decision, *Local Government Board v. Arlidge* (1915), it was held that the inspector's report to the minister after the inquiry did not have to be disclosed. This decision has now been reversed by the statutory rules regulating the procedure of inquiries which are made under the Tribunals and Inquiries Act 1992. These regulations are a statutory embodiment of the rules of natural justice applicable to public inquiries but problems of their interpretation still have to be decided by the courts and, where an inquiry is not regulated by rules, they are still called upon to adapt the rules of natural justice to a policy decision reached by a judicialised procedure. Thus in *Bushell v. Secretary of State for the Environment* (1980) the House of Lords had to decide whether the methodology for making traffic predictions for a new road was a question of fact and therefore open to cross-examination or a matter of policy on which cross-examination was rightly disallowed. In deciding the latter they were very much influenced by the view that a motorway inquiry is part of the policy-making process rather than a trial.

The cases relating to public inquiries were regarded as in a special category by Lord Reid in *Ridge v. Baldwin* (1964), the case which was the springboard from which the expansion of natural justice took off. The courts had before that case limited the application of the rules of natural justice to deprivation of rights rather than privileges and had not applied them to the exercise of wide discretionary powers or the exercise of disciplinary functions. In *Ridge v. Baldwin* the House of Lords declared void the dismissal of the Chief Constable of Brighton because he had not been offered an opportunity to present his case, his dismissal being based on what he himself and the judge had said at his trial on a charge of corruption of which he was acquitted. The court brushed aside the decisions which had narrowed the application of natural justice and, basing itself on earlier decisions, held that where there must be something against a man before he could be dismissed from an office, as in this case, the rules of natural justice had to be observed.

The block having been removed, the way was open to apply the rules of natural justice to an ever expanding category of cases. One of these has been university students who have been held entitled to the benefit of the rules of natural justice before having their course terminated (*R. v. Aston University ex parte Roffey*, 1969) or being suspended from the university (*Glynn v. Keele University*, 1971), although in both cases the courts refused a remedy in the exercise of their discretion because of the facts of the cases. More recently the courts have broken open the prison gates and applied the rules of natural justice in favour of prisoners in the case of the hearing of charges against discipline (*R. v. Visitors of Hull Prison ex parte St Germain*, 1979 and *Leech v. Deputy Governor of Parkhurst Prison*, 1988) and even in respect of the first period (the penal element) of a life sentence for murder (*R. v. Secretary of State for the Home Department ex parte Doody*, 1993). Where issues of national security are involved, the courts have refused to apply the rules of natural justice, *e.g.* in the case of a deportation order based on this ground (*R. v. Home Secretary ex parte Hosenball*, 1977 and *R. v. Secretary of State for the Home Department ex parte Cheblak*, 1991).

Recently, in a landmark decision (*R. v. Secretary of State for the Home Department, ex parte Fayed*, 1998) the Court of Appeal by a majority held that the refusal of citizenship to the Fayed brothers was unfair. Though the British Nationality Act 1981 specifically relieved the Home Secretary from the duty to give reasons, the court held that the applicant had to be given sufficient information about the subject-matter of the decision to enable him to make such submissions as he wished. This did not require the Home Secretary to disclose matters of national security or diplomatic reasons. As a result of the case Mr. Straw, the new Home Secretary, announced that he would in future give reasons when refusing an application for citizenship. Having considered Mohammed Al Fayed's application, he refused it because of a general defect in his character. The Court of Appeal rejected judicial review of this refusal on the grounds that it was not unreasonable.

The *Fayed* case also illustrates how the courts vary the content of the rules of natural justice in accordance with the circumstances of the case. They can include the duty to give reasons, the right to legal representation and the right to cross-examine witnesses at an oral hearing or merely an opportunity to make representations without knowing all the evidence against one or the source of the information. This attenuated form of natural justice is sometimes referred to as a duty to act fairly but these terms are also treated as synonymous. Recently the duty to act fairly has been applied to cases where a person has a "legitimate expectation". This vague concept has been applied to a number of situations such as the revocation of a permit before it has expired, the remission of a sentence and, as we saw, the statement in a Home Office circular of the circumstances when an adopted child would be allowed into this country. The most famous application of the concept was in the GCHQ case when the House of Lords held that the trade unions at GCHQ had a legitimate expectation based on past practice to be consulted about the ban on employees from being members of a trade union. This right to be consulted was, however, in the circumstances of the case negated in the interests of national security. But it was successfully asserted in one of the many cases concerning local government finance, enabling a number of London borough councils to have the decision reducing their grant declared invalid because the minister had refused to hear further representations (*R. v. Secretary of State for the Environment ex parte Brent LBC*, 1982). The victory was pyrrhic for one authority because the minister, having listened to further representations, still withheld the grant (*R. v. Secretary of State for the Environment ex parte Hackney LBC*, 1983). The concept of legitimate expectation has extended the principle of fairness to a category of cases where natural justice had not previously been applied and has thus advanced the cause of open government, though at the expense of slowing down the process of policy-making. This was dramatically illustrated by the judicial review proceedings to halt the pit closures announced by the President of the Board of Trade in October 1992. The court held that the trade unions and their members had a legitimate expectation that the colliery review procedure, which had been agreed after the miners' strike in 1985, would be used and the decision was, therefore, unlawful (*R. v. President of the Board of Trade ex parte NUM etc. Guardian*, December 22, 1992). This was, however, again a pyrrhic victory as in May 1993 the court reversed its earlier decision because no agreement could be reached between British Coal and the NUM on an independent review procedure and British Coal had allowed independent scrutiny of its proposals (*The Times* Law Reports, May 28, 1993). A legitimate expectation to be consulted may also be inapplicable when immediate decisions have to be made. The Law Society's challenge of the regulations cutting the number of people eligible for legal aid failed on this ground (*The Guardian*, June 22, 1993).

A legitimate expectation may also arise from an express promise and such a promise may be held binding on the public authority not only where it relates to matters of procedure, such as consultation, but also on substantive issues. So a health authority who had promised a severely disabled patient a home for life, when moving her to a nursing home from a hospital, were held to have acted unfairly when they later decided to close the home and transfer the patients to the local authority, and their decision was quashed (*R v. North and East Devon Health Authority, ex parte Coughlan*, 2000). In such a case, equivalent to a breach of contract, there would have to be an overriding public interest for such a change of policy. On the other hand, a public authority must be able to change its policy in the public interest even at the expense of a private individual. Thus it was held in *Laker Airways Ltd v. Department of Trade* (1977) that the government was entitled to change its policy about the licence granted to Mr Laker to run Skytrain to the USA, even though he had suffered loss by relying on previous representations, because a government must be allowed to change its policy (Lord Denning dissented on this point). However, the government's policy decision was declared invalid on other grounds.

Similarly, a government may not fetter its own discretion by laying down rules for its exercise unless it is prepared to hear representations from anyone that the rule should be changed or not apply to him. This ensures that discretion is exercised on the facts of each case and was another ground on which the London borough councils won their case against the reduction of their grant, for the minister had refused to listen to any further representations. This rule is the converse of the legitimate expectation rule. One rule is in favour of flexibility, the other is in favour of the status quo.

Thus the courts have fashioned a battery of principles through which they can impose their values on public authorities. The government can by legislation reverse any decision of the courts, but it cannot easily eradicate the principles on which judicial control is based. Perhaps this should be regarded as the true meaning of the rule of law.

PARLIAMENTARY COMMISSIONER FOR ADMINISTRATION

The Parliamentary Commissioner for Administration (PCA) or Ombudsman, as he is popularly called, was set up under the Parliamentary Commissioner Act 1967 in response to pressure which began in 1954 with the Crichel Down affair, the classic illustration of maladministration by civil servants, for which the only remedy was to bring political and parliamentary pressure on the minister who eventually set up an inquiry to investigate the affair, which, as we saw, led to his resignation. Since this machinery cannot be set in motion for every mistake made in a government department, an aggrieved individual is left without a remedy apart from writing to his M.P. The Franks Committee, which was set up in the wake of the Crichel Down affair, was only empowered to consider the workings of tribunals and inquiries and did not, therefore, include the ordinary administrative process of a government department. The catalyst which gave the impetus for the establishment of the PCA was a report commissioned in 1961 by JUSTICE, a private organisation consisting of lawyers, which remodelled the Scandinavian institution of the Ombudsman by reference to the British Comptroller and Auditor General and recommended the creation of a Parliamentary Commissioner for Administration.

The hallmark of the PCA which distinguishes his office from that of the Ombudsman is its parliamentary nature. This is the rationale which underlies the whole institution and gives it its distinctive flavour. It is responsible for one of the main limitations peculiar to the British institution, namely that complaints must come through an M.P. rather than directly from the aggrieved citizen. This has not prevented individuals from approaching the PCA directly and he receives thousands of telephone inquiries and hundreds of letters. Some of these cases are referred to M.P.s and come back to the PCA as formal complaints. M.P.s now forward about 1500 cases annually.

The narrowness of the PCA's jurisdiction is probably the greatest limitation on the office. The complaint must be one of maladministration resulting in injustice in connection with action taken by a government department or other body to which the Act applies, provided it is not in one of the excepted categories listed in the Act. Large areas of administration are thus excluded from the PCA's remit, though the gaps may be filled by other institutions. Thus the exclusion of local authorities is now made good by the establishment of Local Commissioners for Administration in 1974 who perform similar functions *vis-à-vis* local authorities. Complaints against the police are now supervised by the Police Complaints Authority set up under the Police and Criminal Evidence Act 1984. The PCA himself has been appointed as Health Service Commissioner, who since 1973 performs similar functions to the PCA in relation to the National Health Service. Scotland and Wales now each have their own PCA and Ombudsman, respectively. The PCA has been appointed as the first holder of these offices for the time being. Governments have rejected the extension of the PCA's ambit to the nationalised industries on the grounds that they are commercial bodies and have their own complaints machinery. The government in 1985 accepted recommendations to include about 50 quangos within the PCA's jurisdiction including such bodies as the British

Council, the Commission for Racial Equality and Equal Opportunities Commission and the London Docklands Development Corporation, thus increasing the public accountability of these bodies (Parliamentary and Health Service Commissioners Act 1987). Many more bodies have been added since that date. After a long battle the administrative actions of those court and tribunal staff appointed by the Lord Chancellor and the administrative staff of certain tribunals were also brought within the PCA's jurisdiction (Courts and Legal Services Act 1990 and Parliamentary Commissioner Act 1994). The executive agencies which now constitute such a large part of the civil service also fall within the remit of the PCA, as do those functions which have been contracted out to private contractors (Annual Report of the PCA for 1993, para. 8). The PCA would like to see all public bodies which are funded by public money within his jurisdiction unless they are expressly excluded.

Some of the excluded categories of cases have also been the subject of controversy, in particular the exclusion of personnel matters in relation to the armed forces and civil servants. Governments have steadfastly refused to extend the PCA's jurisdiction to these cases on the grounds that other employees do not have access to the PCA for their grievances and that there are other mechanisms available for their redress. The other controversial exclusion is for contractual and other commercial transactions. This excludes the whole area of government contracting, even though this has been used for political purposes as happened when the government blacklisted and refused to give government contracts to those firms which broke its incomes policy from 1975 to 1978. It also bars him from investigating the giving of assistance to industry under wide discretionary powers but includes within his remit assistance which applicants expect to receive (Cmnd. 7449, 1979). There was also controversy over whether Social Fund Officers who make decisions about lump sum payments from the Social Fund come within the PCA's jurisdiction but complaints about the operation of the Social Fund are being investigated.

The main limitation on the PCA's jurisdiction prevents him questioning the merits of a decision taken without maladministration (Parliamentary Commissioner Act 1967, s. 12(3)). Maladministration is not defined in the Act but Mr Crossman when introducing the Bill said it included bias, neglect, inattention, delay, incompetence, ineptitude, perversity, turpitude, arbitrariness. The PCA has now rephrased this catalogue in the

language of the 1990s (Annual Report for 1993, para. 7). More succinctly, the first PCA drew the distinction between the processes
by which the decision was reached and the quality of the decision
itself (H.C. 6, 1967–68). Nevertheless, the distinction is a fine one
and it was further blurred by his following the recommendation
of the select committee, to whom he reports, which wanted him
to exercise jurisdiction over a perverse decision and where an
administrative rule led to hardship (H.C. 350, 1967–68). Some of
the PCA's most famous cases have been on the borderline
between maladministration and the merits of a decision. Among
his first cases were British prisoners of war who had been kept in
German concentration camps and had been refused compensation provided by the German government and distributed by the
Foreign Office. The view had been taken that they did not fall
within the rules which had been drawn up by the Foreign Office
for its distribution. The PCA criticised this decision (H.C. 54,
1967–68) and the complainants were granted compensation by
George Brown, the Foreign Secretary at the time, but he rejected
the PCA's criticisms and questioned whether the PCA's judgment
was better than that of all the Foreign Secretaries who had dealt
with the problem (H.C. Deb., vol. 758, col. 115, February 5, 1968).
Similarly, in the case of Court Line, a company which was given
financial assistance by Mr Benn, the PCA criticised the wording of
the minister's statement to the House of Commons about the
company as misleading (H.C. 498, 1974–75). Again this criticism
was rejected by the minister because these were issues of policy
on which the government had to make a judgment rather than the
PCA (H.C. Deb., vol. 897, col. 582, August 6, 1975). The more
recent *cause célèbre* where the same thing happened was the
Barlow Clowes affair. Investors in the company, who lost their
money when it went into liquidation, claimed that the
Department of Trade and Industry were to blame for licensing the
company, failing to revoke the licence and delaying an investigation into its affairs. The PCA found maladministration because of
the lack of a sufficiently rigorous and enquiring approach by the
Department (H.C. 76, 1989–90). The government rejected this
finding and pointed out that the PCA should not criticise the merits of a decision. Nevertheless it agreed to pay £150 million compensation without admission of fault out of respect for the office
of the PCA (H.C. 99, 1989–90). These cases show the danger of the
PCA stepping outside his jurisdiction and becoming embroiled in
highly controversial political issues. The risk is that he then
becomes a political football who is used by the opposition to

attack the government but whose reports are in consequence rejected by the government as not being within his terms of reference. Nevertheless, these cases are good for his public image.

On the other hand, they weaken his position which is based on acceptance of his reports, not on enforcement. The PCA has no powers except to make reports. The report on the individual case is sent to the M.P. who forwarded the complaint and to the Department and individual who were the subject of the complaint. An annual report and periodical reports with detailed cases are made to the House of Commons where they are referred to the Select Committee on Public Administration. Special reports may be made on *causes célèbres* such as the case of the prisoners of war (*Sachsenhausen* case) and the *Court Line* and *Barlow Clowes* cases. The only back-up power the PCA has, if he thinks that an injustice has not been remedied following his report, is to make a special report to the House of Commons (1967 Act, s. 10(3)). This has happened in only two cases so far, the latest arising out of the blight caused by the planning of the Channel Tunnel Rail Link. After the PCA's special report and a report from the Select Committee, the Conservative government finally agreed to introduce a compensation scheme for those affected to an exceptional degree and the new Labour government confirmed a more generous scheme (H.C. 845 (1997–98)). The rare use of this power does not mean, as we have seen in the *Court Line* case, that his recommendations are always accepted, though this does happen in the vast majority of cases. It does, however, illustrate that the PCA gets his way through persuasion and sometimes negotiation with the Department, which may change its mind during the course of the investigation.

The Select Committee on the PCA, which was set up by the House of Commons and has now been succeeded by the Select Committee on Public Administration, plays an important part in bringing pressure to bear on government departments. It does not reinvestigate individual cases but considers the annual and special reports of the PCA by questioning the departments which are most frequently complained against, *i.e.* the Department of Social Security and the Inland Revenue. It monitors the extent to which complaints have been remedied and how far defects of administration highlighted in the reports have been put right. It is also concerned with reviewing the jurisdiction of the PCA and, as we have seen, has brought about important extensions of his terms of reference. It has conducted a wide-ranging inquiry into the work, powers and jurisdiction of the PCA (H.C. 33–I,

1993–94). It forms the most important pressure group for the PCA, though it has, exceptionally, criticised the PCA himself for delay in handling a complaint which, ironically, is one of the classic illustrations of maladministration (H.C. 312, 1985–86) and has been generally concerned about the length of time taken to resolve complaints.

The average time taken for the investigation of complaints is now under 12 months, as the backlog of complaints has been cleared, and the PCA hopes to reduce this further. Delay is largely the result of the PCA's method of investigation which has been described as a Rolls-Royce method. However, the PCA has gradually modified his procedure. He now tries to settle cases by informal enquiries wherever possible and in over 100 cases annually this leads to a satisfactory conclusion including appropriate redress by the government department. Such cases concentrate more on redress for the individual than on identifying faults in the system of administration. These cases have not been counted as investigations, which take place in only about 20 per cent of cases because most complaints referred to him fall outside his jurisdiction. The PCA has now decided not to draw a rigid distinction between cases which are not and those which are accepted for investigation but to take each case as far as is needed for a just resolution (H.C. 593 (1999–2000)).

His powers of investigation are very wide. He has power to call for information from the minister downwards and he has access to all documents except those relating to the Cabinet (1967 Act, s. 8). The thoroughness of his investigations accounts for the size of his staff (about 100) which is much greater than that of most other ombudsmen. Most of his staff were seconded from the civil service, but more are now on indefinite term contracts. Their working methods are again modelled on the Comptroller and Auditor General's office. Unlike other ombudsmen, the PCA has few lawyers on his staff, although two PCAs have themselves been lawyers in contrast to the others who were civil servants. For the first time the PCA's investigation of a case has been successfully challenged, twice in the same case, for failing to take into account certain considerations — the same ground on which he has made findings of maladministration (*R. v. Parliamentary Commissioner for Administration, ex parte Balchin* (No. 2), 2000).

The parliamentary connection of the PCA profoundly affects the publicity for his office and, therefore, his public image. His individual reports are not given to the press but to the M.P.s who may decide to inform the press. Very few of his cases have become headline news and the PCA himself is hardly a public figure. Whether this is to be regretted or applauded depends on one's perception of his function. The fact that he has unearthed no major scandal even of Crichel Down proportions may be an indication of the quality of the civil service or of the narrowness of his remit. He cannot disclose information obtained for the purpose of his investigation for any other purpose, *e.g.* to the police (1967 Act, s. 11(2)). To change this was said by the then Head of the Civil Service to represent a major change of principle (H.C. 615, 1977–78, para. 35). He has no power, unlike his counterparts abroad, to make an investigation on his own initiative without a complaint. He is not a trouble-shooter who is asked by the government to investigate major issues of public concern, as again happens elsewhere. There are other mechanisms for this purpose, particularly tribunals of inquiry and select committees which sit in public to hear evidence. He cannot, like the courts, quash a decision or order the payment of damages, though in many cases he has secured *ex gratia* compensation for the complainant. He cannot deal with cases where there is a legal remedy unless he is satisfied that it is not reasonable to expect the complainant to resort to it (1967 Act, s. 5(2)). He refused to investigate the cases of haemophiliacs who contracted Aids from blood supplied by the NHS because legal action was being taken (*The Guardian*, August 31, 1990). He told Mr Evans, the former editor of *The Times*, who wanted him to investigate its sale to Mr Murdoch which had not been referred to the Monopolies Commission, that this was a political issue which was not within his powers of investigation (*The Guardian*, February 16, 1984). When he does get drawn into a politically controversial issue he must, as we have seen, tread the tightrope between maladministration and merits. His main function in such cases, if he does investigate, is to establish the facts impartially, for which he has unparalleled powers. Perhaps the PCA's main importance is that he exists. As he pointed out in one of his reports, "Those who are inclined to criticise our public service rather freely would do well to consider what it must be like to live in countries where to criticise a great department of state may be to invite imprisonment or worse" (H.C. 322, 1983–84, para. 1). On the other hand it has been said that the PCA "was a creature of his time but that time has now largely passed." (Ryle and Richards, 1988, p. 199) This was said before the publication of the Citizen's Charter and other specific Charters. Though these may have the effect of complaints being settled without resort to the PCA, he remains as a weapon of last resort and the Charters provide him with useful yardsticks for determining maladministration. The growth of internal complaints mechanisms within departments has, however, caused problems of overlap with the PCA and the proliferation of ombudsmen has led to "Ombudsman fatigue". A review of public sector ombudsmen in England has recommended a collegiate structure embracing the Parliamentary, Health Service and Local Government ombudsman schemes (Cabinet Office, 2000). It has also recommended the abolition of the M.P. filter. The fundamental issue which has to be resolved is whether the PCA is to remain true to his origins as a Parliamentary watchdog who assists M.P.s or to become a public complaints investigation mechanism, though still accountable to Parliament.

ACCOUNTABILITY TO PARLIAMENT

It could be said that there is not one ombudsman but 659, in that every M.P. acts as one, or 22000 if one includes local councillors who perform similar functions in relation to local authorities. It has been estimated that M.P.s take up about 200,000 cases with ministers annually. As we have seen, only a very small proportion (less than 1 per cent) are referred to the PCA for investigation. Most M.P.s try to get the problems of their constituents solved by their own efforts and only refer cases which are too difficult for them or in order to placate their constituents. It has been suggested that it might be desirable if the citizen could ask the PCA directly to investigate, if he is dissatisfied with the ultimate response from his M.P. but this has been rejected by the Select Committee (H.C. 33–I, 1993–94, para. 77). The M.P. will normally first write a letter to the relevant authority. If correspondence does not lead to a solution he can then ask a parliamentary question. In the aftermath of the Scott Report, which criticised ministers and civil servants for giving misleading replies to M.P.s about the supply of arms to Iraq (H.C. 115 (1995–96) Section D)) guidance was drawn up both for ministers and civil servants about answering parliamentary questions. Ministers who knowingly mislead Parliament will be expected to resign, but this will be difficult to prove, as the Scott Report showed. Civil servants in drafting answers to questions should be as open as possible and reasons should be given for the refusal to answer questions by reference to recognised categories. Once a minister has refused to answer a question, the same question cannot be asked again for three months (H.C. 820 (1997–98). There are other restrictions on the asking of questions. Ministers can only be asked about matters which fall within the sphere of their responsibility. This caused problems in relation to the nationalised industries. Under the nationalisation legislation ministers only had certain powers and were not responsible for day-to-day matters. The problem of asking questions on detail was circumvented by phrasing the question in terms of asking the minister to give a general direction about the issue at hand, but even this barred questions about particular complaints. Ministers could always deflect the question as falling within the responsibility of the board if it was on a day-to-day matter. When ministers said that they would not vote their shareholding in privatised companies such as British Aerospace, they were told that they could not disclaim responsibility for a stake which they still owned then and had the power to use (H.C. Deb., vol. 974, col. 70, November 19, 1979). The Westland affair shows that they can certainly not disclaim responsibility for interventions which they do in fact make, provided, of course, that this becomes known. The same rules apply to other quangos over which the minister retains limited powers. M.P.s may also raise grievances on the adjournment debates at the end of each day's sitting and the debates on the adjournment of the House for a specified period such as at Christmas, as well as adjournment debates in Westminster Hall.

Financial accountability to Parliament is through the Comptroller and Auditor General (C & AG) who reports to the Public Accounts Committee. The C & AG audits the accounts of government departments and some quangos and is concerned not just with whether money has been spent legally, _i.e._ in accordance with the Appropriation Act, but whether it has been used economically and efficiently, though he may not question the merits of government policy. On the basis of his reports the Public Accounts Committee questions officials from the Department and in particular the Permanent Secretary who is personally accountable for the expenditure of public money. The political responsibility of the minister is, however, paramount, so that if the Permanent Secretary considers a minister's decision financially irregular or imprudent he must place his objection on record but in the last resort carry out the minister's instructions (H.C. 393, 1971–72, Q. 133). This is what happened in the case of the Pergau dam project in Malaysia for which aid was provided by the government in spite of the objection of the Permanent Secretary (H.C. 155, 1993–94). Such disagreements must now be reported to the

C & AG without delay (Cm 2602, 1994). This procedure was used in the case of the Millennium Dome, where the accounting officer of the Millennium Commission twice received directions from the chairman, *i.e.* the minister, to make additional grants for the Dome (H.C. Deb., vol. 359, col. 834, December 14, 2000).

Governments of both political parties have always resisted allowing the C & AG access to the accounts of the nationalised industries because they argued that this would hinder their freedom to act as commercial bodies. As we have seen, this freedom was much hampered already by ministerial control and it was the desire to preserve accountability to ministers and through them to Parliament which was probably the real stumbling block to granting the C & AG access to the accounts. Similarly, he has no access to the accounts of limited companies in which the government owns some or all of the shares or to whom it gives subsidies. Where public money has been lost, as in the case of the De Lorean car firm in Northern Ireland, he has no access to the accounts of the company, but only to those of the government department, whom he and the Public Accounts Committee can criticise for not monitoring the firm sufficiently (H.C. 127, 1983–84). Again accountability is through the minister and not directly to Parliament. These issues were hotly debated during the passage of the Government Resources and Accounts Act 2000 through Parliament. An amendment passed by the House of Lords to allow the C & AG access to all documents to which a government department has access was diluted, allowing the Treasury by statutory instrument to add categories of documents to which the C & AG would have access (section 25). In this way it will be for the Treasury rather than Parliament to decide to which documents the C & AG has access — another victory for the Executive over Parliament.

In contrast the accounts of local authorities are audited by auditors appointed by the Audit Commission, a body set up by the Local Government Finance Act 1982. Before that date they were appointed by the minister. The auditor can apply to the court for a declaration that the expenditure of a local authority was unlawful (Audit Commission Act 1998, s. 17). The power of the court to make councillors repay money spent unlawfully or wrongfully lost and to disqualify them from holding office has been abolished by the Local Government Act 2000 (section 90). The £26 million surcharge which was imposed on Lady Porter and others arising out of the selling of Westminster City council properties for the electoral advantage of the majority party, which was quashed by the Court of Appeal and is under appeal to the House of Lords, is likely to be the last of its kind (*Porter v. Magill*, 2000).

None of the mechanisms of control and accountability so far examined involves those who are directly affected by the decisions. The consumer councils of the nationalised industries and privatised utilities do have this function of representing the consumer interest. They have now been supplemented by the Citizen's Charter (now Service First) which has as its goal efficiency through setting and monitoring standards for public services, and redress and compensation for the citizen through complaints machinery. Efficiency is becoming a more important control mechanism over public authorities than democratic accountability. Efficiency can also lead to the delivery of services with fewer staff. This is likely to result in more injustice caused by maladministration. The PCA has called on government departments to provide redress in such cases in the interests of fairness and equity (H.C. 593 (1999–2000)).

6

CIVIL LIBERTIES AND THE HUMAN RIGHTS ACT 1998

Dicey (1885, p. 195) gave as his third meaning of the Rule of Law, "that the constitution is pervaded by the rule of law on the ground that the general principles of the constitution (as, for example, the right to personal liberty, or the right of public meeting) are with us the result of judicial decisions determining the rights of private persons in particular cases brought before the courts; whereas under many foreign constitutions the security (such as it is) given to the rights of individuals results, or appears to result, from the general principles of the constitution." What Dicey regarded as the strength of the constitution so far as civil liberties were concerned became criticised as one of its weaknesses and gave rise to the call for the enactment of the European Convention for the Protection of Human Rights and Fundamental Freedoms in the U.K. In order to see how this *volte face* has come about, we will examine how the civil liberties mentioned by Dicey are protected under English law and how they will be safeguarded by the Human Rights Act 1998 which came into force on October 2, 2000.

PERSONAL LIBERTY

Under this heading are usually included freedom from unlawful arrest and detention and unlawful search of one's person or premises and the seizure of one's property. It is no longer true to say as Dicey did that the rights of the individual in this area are the result of judicial decisions because the Police and Criminal Evidence Act 1984 now embodies the law on this subject and judicial decisions will now have to interpret the Act and the codes made under it rather than follow previous decisions. It is to this Act, therefore, that we must look for the powers of the police to arrest and detain individuals, to search their person and premises and to seize property. The Act and judicial decisions lay down the limitations on personal liberty, they do not state the rights of the individual. This is the crucial difference from the European Convention on Human Rights. The rights in English law are implicit, it is the limitations of those rights which must be authorised by law. Dicey saw this as an important element of the rule of law, first because the focus is on the remedy by which the rights are safeguarded rather than the rights themselves. He took as his example the remedy of habeas corpus. Historically this was of profound significance but, though the right to apply for habeas corpus is expressly saved by the 1984 Act (section 51(d)), its scope is subject to the provisions of that Act. Secondly, Dicey pointed out that constitutions containing declarations of rights may be suspended and, similarly, the European Convention on Human Rights (except for certain articles) can be derogated from in time of war or other public emergency threatening the life of the nation (Article 15). The only derogation made by the U.K. which was embodied in the Human Rights Act 1998, will be dropped as a result of changes made by the Terrorism Act 2000 (Section 41 and Schedule 8). On the other hand, the implicit rights of the individual in Britain cannot be abrogated by a stroke of the pen, though an individual remedy such as habeas corpus has been suspended in time of war or emergency.

However, virtually the same result as the suspension of constitutional rights can come about by an Act of Parliament giving wide powers to the government in time of war or emergency to make regulations to secure the public safety and defence of the realm or the supply and distribution of the necessities of life. In both World Wars the government made regulations under these Acts empowering it to detain persons whom it reasonably believed to be of hostile origin and associations, which in effect deprived such persons of the right to habeas corpus (*Liversidge v. Anderson*, 1942). It is, therefore, the substantive law which limits the freedom of the individual and the remedies by which he can protect his freedom which determine the extent of his liberty. The extent to which these will be affected by the Human Rights Act 1998 will be considered later.

Arrest and detention

The Police and Criminal Evidence Act 1984 extended the powers of the police to arrest suspects. The power of summary arrest by a police constable applied to reasonable suspicion of an offence punishable with imprisonment for five years (arrestable offences) and in addition to a number of less serious offences where there were specific statutory provisions for arrest. There was also a common law power of arrest for breach of the peace. The Act has widened the category of arrestable offences by adding certain offences which are not punishable with five years' imprisonment (section 24). But more importantly it now gives a power of summary arrest in the case of *any* offence provided certain conditions are satisfied. These are concerned either with the inability to ascertain the correct name or a satisfactory address of the suspect so that it will be impracticable to bring the person before a court by issuing a summons, or with the prevention of serious mischief such as physical injury to himself or others or loss or damage to property. But the latter grounds also include preventing the commission of an offence against public decency and obstruction of the highway, which gives the police a wide discretion (section 25). The provisions in the Act are peppered with the phrase 'has reasonable grounds' for suspecting or doubting or believing. The reasonableness of the grounds can only be tested afterwards by an action for damages for false imprisonment. Similarly, a person must be told both that he is under arrest and the grounds for his arrest; the arrest is not lawful otherwise (section 28). But again this can only be tested afterwards in an action for damages. Persons who are voluntarily helping the police with their inquiries are free to leave unless arrested (section 29) but there are no provisions for telling persons this except at the stage when they are suspected of an offence (Code C: para. 3.15).

The use of powers of arrest varies greatly between police forces. In *Mohammed-Holgate v. Duke* (1984), an action for wrongful arrest, it was argued that it was unlawful to arrest someone, even if he was reasonably suspected of an arrestable offence, if he was only arrested so that greater pressure could be put on him to confess than if he were interviewed without being arrested. The House of Lords held that, since the police officer had a discretion whether to arrest, once he had reasonable grounds for suspecting an arrestable offence, the exercise of his discretion could not be questioned except on grounds of irrationality (see Chapter 5). This case sanctioned the power of the police to arrest and detain suspects for questioning, provided that there was a power to arrest, before this was explicitly enshrined in the 1984 Act, section 37.

It is now recognised that the primary purpose of detaining a person in police custody after arrest is to obtain from him or through him sufficient evidence to charge him with an offence. The Act and the code made under it are an attempt to hold the balance between giving the police powers to hold the suspect and question him and safeguarding the rights of the individual. Whether the balance is tipped too far in one direction or the other is a matter of judgment that can only be reached after examining the provisions. There is much dispute whether the provisions increased the powers of the police before the Act but the answer is inconclusive because the powers were so uncertain, which was one of the main reasons for passing the Act. The Act and the code are a mixture of police powers and safeguards for the individual, the crucial issue is the extent to which the safeguards are enforceable.

Where the police do not have sufficient evidence to charge the arrested person they may detain him for questioning for up to 24 hours with reviews by a superior officer after six hours and nine hours thereafter. At the end of that period he must either be charged with an offence or released (section 41). However, in the case of a serious arrestable offence which is rather widely defined in the Act (section 116), the period of detention can be extended up to 36 hours and this can be extended by a magistrates' court for two further periods of up to 36 hours to a maximum of 96 hours (sections 42–44). This maximum period is longer than that allowed by any common law country but it must be set against the statistics obtained by the Royal Commission on Criminal Procedure (Cmnd. 8092, 1981, para. 3.96) that 75 per cent of all suspects are dealt with in six hours and 95 per cent within 24 hours; only 0.4 per cent were found to have been held for 72 hours or more. A study done since the Act confirms these figures: 76 per cent of detainees were dealt with within six hours, less than 1 per cent were detained more than 24 hours and warrants for further detention beyond 36 hours were sought in only 0.2 per cent of cases (Zander, 1990, p. 91). The limits on detention can be enforced by habeas corpus if the practical problems of making an application for the writ can be overcome and an action for damages for wrongful detention could be brought afterwards (see *Roberts v. Chief Constable of the Cheshire Constabulary*, 1999). The remedies to enforce the other safeguards are not so clear.

When a person is arrested he is given into the charge of a custody officer, who must be of the rank of sergeant or above and who is responsible for ensuring that persons in detention are treated in accordance with the Act and the code made under it (sections 36 and 39) and that a custody record is kept for each person in accordance with the provisions of the Act and the code which lay down what must be recorded, when and by whom. This is to ensure that the procedures laid down are followed correctly and that the safeguards for the treatment of individuals are being observed. But failure to observe these provisions would not make the detention unlawful. There is as yet no independent investigation of complaints against the police, though the Act establishes an independent body, the Police Complaints Authority, to supervise the investigation of complaints (Part IX) (now Police Act 1996, Part IV) and reform of the whole system involving independent investigations of the most serious complaints has been announced (Complaints Against the Police — A New System, Home Office, 2000) and is being enacted. There are, however, other safeguards in the Act and the code.

The Act (section 56) gives a person detained in custody the right on request to have someone of his choice informed that he is being detained. This right can be delayed for up to 36 hours in the case of a person detained for a serious arrestable offence if there are reasonable grounds for fearing that evidence will be interfered with or other suspects will be alerted. Under the code he must be informed of this right. More importantly the Act (section 58) gives a right to a detained person to consult a solicitor privately on request. Again this right may be delayed for up to 36 hours for the same reasons, and again under the code he must be informed of this right. Studies done for the Royal Commission indicated that before the Act, when the right was not statutory, few suspects asked to see a solicitor and most seem to have been refused their request, but they also found that few police forces took adequate steps to make suspects aware of their rights (Cmnd. 8092, 1981, para. 4.83). Perhaps the most important change made by the Act is the extension of the duty solicitor scheme to police stations, so that free legal advice will be available round the clock to suspects. Duty solicitors are now appointed in accordance with the provisions of the Access to Justice Act 1999 to ensure that those who give advice are competent. Under the code a person may not be interviewed until he has received legal advice, where he has requested it, except where the 36 hour delay applies or he has agreed in writing or where it would unreasonably delay the investigation, which gives further discretion to the police. The solicitor must also be allowed to be present at the interview. Sixty per cent of suspects still do not ask for legal advice (Zander, 1999, p. 69). Arguably the most important safeguards for suspects contained in the Act are in section 60 which lays a duty on the Home Secretary to require interviews with suspects to be tape-recorded. In pursuance of this section the Home Secretary issued a code of practice on tape-recording in 1988 and tape-recording of interviews in the case of offences triable by jury was made compulsory from January 1, 1992.

With these safeguards in place it is tempting to ask why it was found necessary to set up another Royal Commission on Criminal Justice in 1991 only 10 years after the report of the previous one, whose recommendations gave rise to the 1984 Act. The answer lies in the series of miscarriages of justice which came to light from the late 1980s onwards of which the Maguire Seven, the Guildford Four and the Birmingham Six were the most prominent. These have been followed by a series of other miscarriages of justice such as the Tottenham Three, the Cardiff Three, the *Judith Ward* case and the *Stefan Kiszko* case. Some of these cases but not all predated the safeguards introduced by the 1984 Act. A number of the cases involved terrorism to which even now the same safeguards would not apply. What are the defects in the 1984 Act exposed by these cases and others and to what extent would they be cured by the recommendations of the Royal Commission (Cm 2263, 1993)?

The key to these problems lies in the sanctions for enforcing the safeguards contained in the Act. Since the questioning of suspects is designed to obtain evidence from them it is the admissibility of such evidence, where the Act or the codes have been breached, that is crucial. The Act provides that a confession is inadmissible where it was obtained by oppression or where anything was said or done which was likely to render it unreliable (section 76). In addition evidence may be excluded where it appears, having regard to all the circumstances, including the way it was obtained, it would have such an adverse effect on the fairness of the proceedings that the court should not admit it (section 78). It has been held in *R. v. Samuel* (1988) that wrongful denial of access to a solicitor did fall within section 78 so as to render the confession inadmissible, though in a later case the court held the confession admissible, where the defendant had stated in evidence that he knew his rights and, therefore, the presence of the solicitor was not crucial (*R. v. Alladice*, 1988). There have been a plethora of decisions since the Act determining when breaches of the Act rendered confessions inadmissible. Many of the miscarriages of justice turned on tainted confessions which were admitted at the trials and were sometimes the only evidence. Two possible remedies have been rejected by successive Royal Commissions. The first, to adopt the American exclusionary rule which renders inadmissible illegally obtained evidence was rejected in 1981. The second, to make corroboration of confessions essential was rejected in 1993 (Cm 2263, Chapter 4), though only by a majority.

The reverse case where parents who refused to answer any questions about the death of their baby were not prosecuted because of the absence of any independent witnesses (*The Guardian*, February 25, 1993) raises equally fundamental questions about our criminal justice system. It calls into question the right to silence, *i.e.* the rule which prohibits the refusal to answer questions by the police to be used to infer guilt or to be commented on adversely at the trial. Both Royal Commissions have recommended the retention of this fundamental right against self-incrimination, but the government rejected this recommendation in 1993. The Criminal Justice and Public Order Act 1994 (Part III) allows the court or jury to draw such inferences as appear proper from the accused's failure, when questioned by the police, to mention a fact on which he relies in his defence which he could reasonably have been expected to mention. The same inferences may be drawn from his failure to give evidence at his trial and from the failure of an arrested person to account for objects, substances or marks, or his presence at a particular place. These provisions were modelled on those in force in Northern Ireland. The Royal Commission was concerned with the possibility of more miscarriages of justice, the government with the obtaining of more convictions. The House of Lords' attempt to find a compromise solution to allow inferences to be drawn from silence but provide better safeguards for those being questioned, resulted in an amendment to make a caution obligatory before questioning by the police but an amendment which would have required the questioning to take place in a police station with the attendant safeguards was defeated (H.L. Deb., vol. 556, col. 1386 seq., July 7, 1994). However, where the accused was in a police station when being questioned, he must be allowed an opportunity to consult a solicitor before adverse inferences can be drawn from his silence. (Youth Justice and Criminal Evidence Act 1999, s. 58). This provision was enacted specifically to comply with the Human Rights Act 1998.

No safeguards can be foolproof against the fabrication of evidence by the police which was responsible for some of the miscarriages of justice, particularly those in which the West Midlands CID was involved which was disbanded. The only remedy in such cases must be retrospective, namely the quashing of the conviction and prosecution or disciplinary proceedings and an action for damages against the police. In the case of the Guildford Four, though the convictions were quashed, the three police officers who were prosecuted were acquitted. In the case of the Birmingham Six the judge ordered the prosecution to be dropped because the intensity of media publicity made it impossible to have a fair trial. The double jeopardy rule has prevented disciplinary proceedings for an offence for which a prosecution has been brought. This rule has been abolished by the Police Act 1996.

Many millions of pounds of compensation have been paid to victims of miscarriages of justice and the sums paid for miscarriages of justice arising out of the arms to Iraq affair alone have already cost taxpayers millions of pounds (*The Guardian*, October 31, 2000). The Criminal Cases Review Commission set up under the Criminal Appeal Act 1995 may refer a conviction to the Court of Appeal where it considers there is a real possibility that it would not be upheld because of an argument or evidence not raised in the proceedings. The Commission can investigate the cases itself or appoint investigating officers such as police officers. The Commission has been far less reluctant to refer cases to the Court of Appeal than the Home Office, which was previously responsible for referrals, so that miscarriages of justice stand more chance of being rectified after they have taken place, though the Commission still has a large backlog of cases.

Stop and search power

There is power under the Police and Criminal Evidence Act 1984 (Part I) to stop and search persons and vehicles in a public place on reasonable suspicion of finding stolen goods or offensive weapons. This power previously existed only in certain areas of the country which had obtained special legislation in private Acts of Parliament. It is a very controversial power which has had particular impact on some sections of the community such as young black people and which Lord Scarman pinpointed as a contributory factor in sparking off the Brixton disorders (Cmnd. 8427, 1981, para. 3.27). The code of practice on stop and search powers now lays down guidance on what does and does not constitute reasonable suspicion and states explicitly that colour or style of dress can never by themselves be grounds for reasonable suspicion. But breach of the code is not a crime nor does it give rise to an action for damages by itself, though it must be taken into account in any proceedings to which it is relevant (section 67), which would be an action for assault where the stop and search was unlawful. The use by the police of stop and search powers was criticised by the Macpherson report on the death of Stephen Lawrence for discriminating against black people (Cm 4262, 1999) and since then the powers have been used less frequently but have been better targeted. There is a new power in the Criminal Justice and Public Order Act 1994 (section 60) to stop and search persons and vehicles for a maximum of 30 hours where the police reasonably believe serious violence may take place in an area.

Search and seizure

The other main police power under the Police and Criminal Evidence Act 1984 is to enter and search premises and seize property. From a historical point of view this is perhaps the greatest infringement of individual liberty because the great constitutional case proclaimed in ringing tones the principle that an Englishman's home is his castle, "The great end, for which men entered into society, was to secure their property" (*Entick v. Carrington*, 1765). This eighteenth-century case decided that it was illegal for the Home Secretary to issue a warrant authorising entry of a person's house to search for and seize his papers to find evidence of seditious libel. Since that case was decided, the power to search for evidence of an offence or for unlawful articles was conferred by a number of statutes, but there were glaring gaps such as the lack of a power to issue a search warrant to find evidence in the case of murder. This was highlighted in the case of *Ghani v. Jones* (1970) where the police managed to obtain the passports and letters from persons they suspected of being implicated in a murder but were ordered to hand them back by Lord Denning because they had not shown reasonable grounds for believing that the plaintiffs were implicated in the crime or that the documents were material evidence to prove commission of the crime. In that case Lord Denning laid down sweeping propositions of law about search and seizure of property for which there was little authority. This confused and haphazard state of the law cried out for reform which is now embodied in the 1984 Act.

The Act for the first time gave a general power to the police to obtain a warrant from a magistrate to enter premises and to search for evidence where they have reasonable grounds to believe that a serious arrestable offence has been committed and that this was the only practicable way to obtain the evidence (section 8). The premises may be those of a third party who is not suspected of any offence. When the Bill was first published there was an outcry from the caring professions, *e.g.* doctors and social workers, who feared the possibility of their confidential records being ransacked to find evidence of a crime. As a result the second Bill was substantially modified so as to exclude-from its ambit altogether confidential personal records as well as confidential journalistic material in addition to communications between a client and his legal adviser which had been previously excluded. Other confidential or journalistic material can only be searched for by obtaining an order from a circuit judge (section 9).

These powers have been used extensively to order the media, who cover demonstrations where disturbances take place, to hand over to the police photographs or film to help with the identification of suspects. The media have unsuccessfully objected to such orders because of the danger of journalists being attacked by demonstrators to avoid detection but in a landmark decision, *The Guardian* and *The Observer* succeeded in quashing an order to produce documents relating to David Shayler, a former MI5 officer being investigated for disclosure of official secrets. In a ringing affirmation of the common law principle that an Englishman's home is his castle, Judge L.J. said, "Premises are not to be entered by the forces of authority or the state to deter or diminish, inhibit or stifle the exercise of an individual's right to free speech or the press of its freedom to investigate and inform" (*R (Bright) v. Central Criminal Court*, 2001, p. 681). The common law anticipated the Human Rights Act 1998 by nearly two and a half centuries.

Under the Prevention of Terrorism Act 1989 (Schedule 7), now replaced by the Terrorism Act 2000 (Schedule 5) there are even more draconian powers under which orders can be made to hand over material which would be excluded under the 1984 Act, namely confidential journalistic material such as the sources from which information was obtained. Channel 4 were found guilty of contempt of court for refusing to comply with such an order, which would have endangered the life of an informant whose identity was not disclosed in a programme about terrorism in Northern Ireland (*The Guardian*, August 1, 1992).

No warrant or order is necessary to search the premises in which a person was arrested (section 32) for evidence relating to the offence or to search the premises occupied by someone arrested for an arrestable offence after his arrest (section 18) for evidence relating to that offence or a related or similar offence. Once lawfully on the premises, the police may take anything which they reasonably believe is evidence of any offence whatsoever in order to prevent the evidence being lost or destroyed (section 19). These provisions put into statutory form some of the most controversial statements made by Lord Denning in *Ghani v.*

Jones (1970) and even go beyond them. They encourage the police to go on fishing expeditions, looking for evidence which is not within the warrant or is not connected with the offence for which a person is arrested. Though such searches may be illegal under the provisions of the Act (sections 16(8), 18(3) and 32(3), evidence so found would not be inadmissible unless it fell within the provision for the exclusion of unfair evidence (section 78). The Royal Commission would have excluded evidence obtained by an illegal search (Cmnd. 8092, 1981, para. 3.49) to minimise fishing expeditions. The possibility of an action for damages after the event against the police and possible disciplinary proceedings are not a sufficient deterrent. The Englishman's castle has let down its drawbridge for the police.

Telephone tapping and surveillance

The police have other means of obtaining evidence of an offence which are subject to even fewer safeguards than is the searching of premises. Telephone tapping was, until April 1986, when the Interception of Communications Act 1985 came into force, carried out under the authority of a warrant issued by a Secretary of State in accordance with guidelines which had been laid down by him. When the legality of this procedure was challenged in *Malone v. Metropolitan Police Commissioner* (1979) the judge did not follow *Entick v. Carrington* (1765) and hold such warrants illegal because no property right was infringed by telephone tapping. He held that "it can lawfully be done simply because there is nothing to make it unlawful" (pp. 733–34). The principle, which can be regarded as an important safeguard for the rights of the individual, had a diametrically opposite result here. *Malone* took his case to the European Court of Human Rights (1984) where it was held that the United Kingdom had broken the European Convention on Human Rights, Article 8, under which everyone has the right to respect for his private and family life, his home and his correspondence. The court held that the minimum degree of legal protection to which citizens are entitled under the rule of law in a democratic society was lacking.

To comply with the judgment, the Interception of Communications Act 1985 was passed by Parliament. This Act has now been repealed and replaced by Part I of the Regulation of Investigatory Powers Act 2000. It retains the broad framework of the 1985 Act for the interception of communications whilst extending it with some exceptions to private networks linked to a public telecommunications system and to the plethora of new telecommunications and mail delivery systems. It makes telephone tapping a criminal offence except where it is carried out by consent or under the authority of a warrant issued by the Secretary of State in accordance with the provisions of the Act (section 1). The Act lays down in broad terms the grounds on which warrants may be issued, their scope and duration and the procedure for issuing them, as well as other safeguards (sections 5–16). Some changes have been made to ensure compliance with Article 8 of the European Convention on Human Rights. A tribunal of lawyers has been set up to whom complaint can be made by someone who thinks his telephone has been tapped, but they can only say whether or not they have made a determination in favour of the complainant (section 68). They cannot tell him whether there was a warrant issued and whether this complied with the Act or whether there was illegal tapping without a warrant for which a prosecution can be brought only with the consent of the Director of Public Prosecutions. The decisions of the tribunal cannot be challenged in any court (section 67) nor can any proceedings be brought before a court challenging the legality of a warrant or the legality of telephone tapping except where there is a prosecution for illegal tapping (sections 17 and 18). It would, therefore, now be impossible for someone in the position of *Malone* to bring his case before a court. It was, however, possible for the Campaign for Nuclear Disarmament (CND) to challenge the legality of a warrant allegedly issued by the Home Secretary to tap the phone of its vice-president before the Act came into force. The judge rejected the application because he held that the warrant had been lawfully issued on grounds of national security. He held that he could review the case even though it involved a question of national security and went on to hold that in accordance with the doctrine of legitimate expectation (see chapter 5) ministers were bound by their own guidelines (*R. v. Secretary of State for the Home Department ex parte Ruddock*, 1987).

The 1985 Act was used as the model when the Security Service (MI5) and the Secret Intelligence Service (MI6) and GCHQ were placed on a statutory footing by the Security Service Act 1989 and the Intelligence Services Act 1994. The Services were given statutory authority to apply for warrants from the relevant Secretary of State to enter or interfere with property, if he thinks it is necessary to obtain information for the discharge of their functions and the action is proportionate to what it seeks to achieve (Regulation of Investigatory Powers Act 2000, section 74). These functions are defined as the protection of national security and in particular its protection against threats from espionage, terrorism and actions intended to overthrow parliamentary democracy by political, industrial or violent means and to safeguard the economic well-being of the U.K. against threats from outside Britain (MI5) and to obtain information about persons outside the U.K. in the interests of national security (MI6). Action in support of the police in the prevention and detection of serious crime was added for MI5 in 1996. The exercise of the Secretary of State's power to issue warrants is overseen by the Intelligence Services Commissioner, who must be or have been a judge, and the Tribunal consisting of lawyers to whom complaints can be made about conduct by any of the intelligence services in relation to the complainant or his property. The Tribunal can ask the Commissioner for assistance and award compensation and quash a warrant and order the destruction of any files or make any other order they think fit but they can only review conduct to the same extent as a court would on an application for judicial review (section 67).

The Regulation of Investigatory Powers Act 2000, Part II now provides similar procedures for authorising "intrusive surveil-lance" by the Security and Secret Intelligence Services. This covers surveillance inside residential premises or a private vehicle or by placing a device outside. It requires a warrant from the Secretary of State and oversight by the Intelligence Services Commissioner and the Tribunal. However, authorisation of such intrusive surveillance by the police or Customs and Excise is given by the Chief Officer but, except in urgent cases, it will not take effect until approved by a Surveillance Commissioner, who must be or have been a judge. Covert surveillance other than intrusive surveillance can be authorised by designated persons within specified public authorities (Schedule I). This is also subject to the oversight of the Chief Surveillance Commissioner and the Tribunal to whom complaints can be made.

The Tribunal can quash a warrant or authorisation and grant compensation but failure to obtain an authorisation or a warrant does not as such make the action unlawful (section 80). This must now be read subject to the Human Rights Act 1998, s. 6, which makes it unlawful to act in contravention of the European Convention on Human Rights which embodies the right of privacy (Article 8). However, as we have seen, evidence obtained unlawfully is not inadmissible unless it falls within the provisions for the exclusion of unfair evidence. In *R. v. Khan* (1996) it was held that evidence obtained by an unlawful bugging device was not inadmissible but this was decided before the Human Rights Act. The exclusionary rule would now have to be considered in the context of the right to a fair trial under Article 6. However, they are both governed by the same criterion of fairness, so that the decision is likely to be the same (*R. v. P.*, 2001).

No complaint about the interception of communications has been upheld by the Tribunal because in only a handful of the complaints had interception been carried out by a Government agency and these cases were covered by a warrant (Cm 4368, 1999, para. 1.9). Similarly, no complaint has been upheld by the Tribunal against the Security Service or Secret Intelligence Service. This could be seen as a complete vindication of these agencies but it would carry more conviction if there were more open accountability for the security services.

The Intelligence Services Act 1994 (section 10) provided for a Committee of nine members drawn from both Houses of Parliament to examine the expenditure, administration and policy of MI5, MI6 and GCHQ. They are appointed by the Prime Minister after consultation with the Leader of the Opposition and can be dismissed by him at any time. Unlike other Parliamentary Committees it reports annually to the Prime Minister rather than directly to Parliament. Though the Prime Minister has to lay the report before Parliament, he can exclude from the report matter which he thinks would be prejudicial to the discharge of the functions of the security services. Also the Committee cannot obtain information defined as sensitive in the Act, *e.g.* operational matters, which neither the Secretary of State nor the director of one of the security services considers it safe to disclose. Further, the Secretary of State can prevent disclosure on the same grounds on which he withholds information from departmental Select Committees of the House of Commons (*supra*, Chapter 2) but not on grounds of national security alone. The Committee does not have the usual power of departmental committees to call for evidence, except from the heads of the security services, but in a special investigation of the handling of information supplied by the Russian defector (Mitrokhin) undertaken at the request of the Home Secretary, the Committee was given unparalleled access to material beyond that of a Select Committee, including advice to ministers (H.C. Deb., vol. 352, col. 471, June 22, 2000). The Committee has also been able to appoint an Investigator who can inspect all documents connected with an investigation and interview key personnel. He submits his report to the Committee without disclosing operationally sensitive information. The

Committee hopes that his appointment will establish public confidence in the oversight system (Cm 4532, 1999).

FREEDOM OF SPEECH AND PUBLIC ASSEMBLY

Dicey said of the right to free speech, "Freedom of discussion is then, in England, little else than the right to write or say anything which a jury consisting of twelve shopkeepers think it expedient should be said or written" (p. 246). He was, of course, referring to the law of libel. But Dicey was mainly concerned in his discussion of freedom of speech to contrast freedom of the press in Britain with that in France. His basic argument was that the press in Britain was subject to the ordinary law of the land and there was no special press law providing for censorship or giving the press special privileges. In essence that is true today, though, as we have seen, journalistic material is given a special status under the Police and Criminal Evidence Act 1984. Journalists, having obtained these special provisions, later had second thoughts for the reasons given by Dicey, because it singled them out for special treatment.

There are many other legal restrictions on freedom of speech both at common law and by statute apart from the law of libel. Increasingly today individuals want to exercise freedom of speech not in isolation but together with their fellow citizens in marches and demonstrations. This is when the right has to be balanced against public order and the rights of other citizens to go about their business. Mass picketing during industrial disputes raises similar issues. The law which holds the balance between these conflicting freedoms is now mostly contained in the Public Order Act 1986 and the Criminal Justice and Public Order Act 1994 (Part V) which embody in statutory form with some modifications the common law public order offences of riot, rout, unlawful assembly and affray and also re-enact and amend the statutory offences dealing with processions and public assemblies previously contained in the Public Order Act 1936.

The Public Order Act 1986, like the Police and Criminal Evidence Act 1984, contains restrictions on the freedom of the individual; it does not state the right of the individual to assemble peacefully. This is now contained in the Human Rights Act 1998 (Schedule I, Article 11).

The problem of balancing the freedom to assemble against public order is not a new one. It is epitomised in the old case of *Beatty v. Gillbanks* (1882) where the Salvation Army in Weston-super-Mare were wont to march on a Sunday with a band and banners flying. They were opposed by the Skeleton Army who were antagonistic to their views. Fights ensued and the Salvation Army were told not to march. When they persisted despite being asked by the police to disperse, their leaders were arrested and charged with unlawful assembly. On appeal they were held not guilty because the disturbance of the peace was the fault of their opponents and had not been caused by them. This case was distinguished in the later case of *Duncan v. Jones* (1936) where the facts are closer to the problems of our times. Mrs Duncan wanted to hold a meeting to protest about a repressive Bill, then before Parliament, outside a training centre for the unemployed. On a previous occasion a meeting in the same place addressed by Mrs Duncan had led to disturbances in the training centre. The police asked her to hold the meeting a little distance away; she refused and was arrested. She was convicted of obstructing the police in the execution of their duty. Much ink has been spilt over the attempt to reconcile these cases. This is now merely a matter of historical significance. Under the Public Order Act 1986 the Salvation Army would not be guilty of the offence of violent disorder (section 2) because they did not use or threaten violence nor would they be guilty of the offence of using threatening, abusive or insulting words or behaviour which is intended or likely to cause fear of or to provoke immediate violence (section 4). The law on obstruction of the police has not been changed but the police have paid damages to protesters who were wrongfully arrested without a warrant for this offence (*The Guardian*, August 10, 1996). More importantly, what the cases illustrate is the eternal difficulty of reconciling freedom of speech and meeting with public order and in consequence the problems of making and applying laws to hold the balance between them. This is particularly true at times of political and economic unrest and it is no coincidence that the first Public Order Act in 1936 was passed because of disturbances resulting from fascist marches and that the second Public Order Act was passed in 1986 in the aftermath of inner-city riots, the mass picketing during the miners' strike and mass demonstrations by protest groups. Part V of the 1994 Act is concerned with hunt saboteurs and mass protests as well as "raves", squatters and New Age Travellers.

In view of this it is not surprising that the legislation tips the balance further in favour of public order and against freedom of meeting. The government recognised in its White Paper preceding the 1986 Act (Cmnd. 9510, 1985, para. 1.9) that tightening of the law cannot by itself prevent all disorder and that after disorder has broken out the problem is not a shortage of legal powers but enforcement. This is a matter of practical policing and raises questions of equipment and tactics. More importantly, in the case of large-scale disorders, such as the Brixton and other inner-city riots, it raises questions of social policy, particularly towards ethnic minorities, as Lord Scarman stressed in his historic report on the Brixton disorders (Cmnd. 8427, 1981, Part VI). It is in the provisions which give the police powers to prevent disorder that the Public Order Act 1986 tips the balance further against the freedom of speech and assembly.

One of the main new provisions in the Act is section 11 which makes it an offence for those organising a procession to demonstrate for or against a cause or to publicise it or to mark or commemorate an event, not to give six days' advance notice to the police unless this is not reasonably practicable, as in the case of spontaneous demonstrations. This provision is new only in the sense that it applies to the whole country, whereas previous provisions for advance notice only applied in certain areas. It has been argued that the provision is unnecessary as the police usually know in advance about major processions, though this is not so in a minority of cases. The giving of notice is seen as providing a trigger for discussions between the police and the organisers about the manner of conducting the march so as to make the exercise of the statutory powers regulating it unnecessary. On the other hand, where there was no prior knowledge of the march by the police, it would alert them in time to use their powers. It is interesting that a similar provision for static demonstrations and meetings was ruled out by the government for the purely practical reason of generating too much work for the police.

One of the most controversial provisions in the Act was the extension of the powers of the police to impose conditions on a procession (section 12). Though the formal power to give directions imposing conditions which existed under the 1936 Act was rarely used, the existence of the power enables the police to negotiate with the organisers, and the wider the power, the stronger is the bargaining position of the police. The main extension has been in the tests which have to be satisfied before conditions can be imposed. Under the 1936 Act the chief officer of police had to have reasonable grounds for apprehending that the procession might result in serious public disorder. To this the 1986 Act adds reasonable belief of serious damage to property, serious disruption to the life of the community or that the purpose of the organisers is the intimidation of others. These tests widen the power greatly and if used to the full extent could bring almost any large procession within its scope. In theory the exercise of the power could be tested in the courts but in practice the courts have been reluctant to substitute their judgment for that of the police in this area. The conditions which may be imposed are those which appear necessary to the chief constable to prevent disorder, damage, disruption or intimidation, including prescribing the route. It is also now made explicit that conditions can be imposed during the march as well as in advance and the power can then be exercised by the most senior police officer present who could be of junior rank. Failure to comply with a condition knowingly is an offence for the organisers and those taking part and they may be summarily arrested. These powers were deployed to prevent fuel protestors driving lorries into York and the centre of London. (*The Guardian*, November 10 and 11, 2000).

Even more controversial has been the extension of this power to impose conditions to public assemblies (section 14). The criteria for the exercise of the power are the same as for processions, and conditions may be imposed as to the place, the duration and the number of persons who may take part. This provision will for the first time give the police a specific statutory power to limit the number of pickets and where they stand, provided that one of the criteria for imposing conditions applies, which in the case of mass picketing would almost certainly be the case. Failure to comply knowingly will be an offence for which one can be summarily arrested. If the powers under this provision were used to the full extent they would enable the police to exercise control over almost any sizeable demonstration. To fall within the provisions the assembly must be of 20 or more people and be held in a public place which is wholly or partly open to the air. This definition carefully excludes private land to which the public is not admitted, and much pressure was brought on the government to extend the Act to trespassers on private land. At a late stage in the Bill the government finally succumbed to pressure and tabled an amendment to give the police power to direct trespassers to leave land if they reasonably believe that two or more trespassers intend to reside there for any period, that the occupier has taken reasonable steps to get them to leave and that they have caused damage to property or used threatening words or behaviour or have brought twelve or more vehicles on to the land. Failure to obey such a direction or return within three months is a criminal offence (section 39). This section has been considerably widened by Part V of the 1994 Act. Not only has the number of vehicles been reduced to six but there is now power for the police to seize and remove vehicles where a direction to leave the land is in force. Also, a local authority can give a direction to leave to anyone residing in a vehicle on a highway or unoccupied land as well as trespassers on occupied land. A magistrates' court can order removal of a vehicle which remains in contravention of such a direction. These powers have been used vigorously but have usually only succeeded in moving the trespassers from one piece of land to another.

These provisions to issue directions to leave land have been used as the model in the 1994 Act for controlling "raves", *i.e.* concerts of 100 or more people in the open air at night which are likely to cause serious distress to local residents, the music being defined as including, "the emission of a succession of repetitive beats". Again the police are given the power to seize and remove vehicles or sound equipment where a direction to leave the land is in force and even to stop persons on the way to a "rave" within five miles of the site and direct them not to proceed. Failure to obey a direction is an offence.

Similarly, the power to issue directions to leave the land can be used against those committing a new offence of aggravated trespass, which is aimed at those who trespass on land in the open air to intimidate, obstruct or disrupt any lawful activity, *e.g.* hunt saboteurs or motorway protestors. This provision goes furthest towards turning trespass into a criminal offence. It was used extensively against those protesting against the Newbury by-pass but only about half of those prosecuted were convicted and only four of those convicted were imprisoned (*The Guardian*, December 8, 1998).

The 1994 Act also breaks new ground by giving the police power for the first time to apply for a ban on certain assemblies, modelled on the power for banning public processions which has existed since 1936. The assembly must be of at least 20 people trespassing on land in the open air including a highway and either be likely to seriously disrupt the life of the community, or to cause significant damage to land or buildings of historical, architectural, archaeological or scientific importance. The ban cannot exceed four days or an area of more than five miles radius. These provisions were tailor-made to give the police further powers to deal with the annual demonstrations at Stonehenge during the summer solstice. However, in the landmark decision of *DPP v. Jones* (1999) the House of Lords quashed a conviction for disobeying an order prohibiting assemblies within four miles of Stonehenge for four days. There was an assembly of 21 people peacefully demonstrating on a grass verge which was part of the highway. They were not obstructing the highway. The House of Lords by a majority of three judges with two dissenters held that there was a right to use the highway for peaceful assembly as long as it was reasonable and did not obstruct the highway. This overturned a long line of authority which held that the highway could only be used for passing to and fro and rights incidental thereto. Though the case was decided before the Human Rights Act 1998 came into force on October 2, 2000, it establishes the right to peaceful assembly on the highway subject to limitations in the public interest and thus anticipates Article 11 of the European Convention on Human Rights coming into operation.

For several years the police used their powers under section 13 of the Public Order Act 1986 (a re-enactment of the provision in the 1936 Act) to ban processions within a certain radius of Stonehenge. The power can only be used where the chief constable reasonably believes that the power to impose conditions on a procession will not be sufficient to prevent serious public disorder. In exercising this power the chief constable must take into account the mutual aid arrangements whereby he can call on assistance from other police forces. He can then apply to the local authority or in London to the Home Secretary for an order banning all processions or a class of procession for up to three months. The order can only be made with the consent of the Home Secretary both in London and elsewhere. There is no power to ban a specific procession because of the danger that this could lead to accusations of political bias. This does, however, mean that, for example, the National Front can stop all other marches by announcing that they will hold a march which as a result of counter-demonstrations is likely to result in serious public disorder. This has happened on a number of occasions and banning orders increased in the early 1980s. Lord Scarman would have liked a power to ban a specific march if there were reasonable grounds for believing that the march was a threat to public order and likely to stir up racial hatred (Cmnd. 8427, 1981, para. 7.48). There is no such provision in the 1986 Act which does, however, make the law relating to incitement to racial hatred more effective by giving for the first time a power of summary arrest in such a case (section 18) and the 1994 Act added such a power for the offence of distributing racist literature.

The legislation contains no provision for charging the organisers of a demonstration with the cost of policing it. The practical difficulties involved would be very great, but reconciling freedom of speech with public order can be expensive. The policing of Stonehenge during the summer solstice in 1992 cost £200,000 (*The Guardian*, June 18, 1993) and the cost of policing the protests over the Newbury by-pass was over three and a half million pounds just to clear the route and cost up to £50 million to guard (*The Guardian*, April 19, 1996 and December 12, 2000).

Probably the most important common law power which the police retain is to prevent imminent breaches of the peace and arrest those responsible. This power was greatly extended during the miners' strike when miners were stopped at a road block on the M1 and were arrested when they tried to proceed. Their conviction for obstructing the police was upheld because on the facts the police acted reasonably in forming the opinion that there was a real risk of a breach of the peace in close proximity both in place and time, there being four pits within five miles of the road block (*Moss v. McLachlan, The Times*, November 29, 1984). That this case was hailed as a limitation on police powers shows how much the police had stretched their powers in setting up other road blocks. The road blocks set up during the industrial dispute at the News International plant at Wapping were justified by the police under the Metropolitan Police Act 1839, section 52 which gives power to direct constables to keep order and prevent obstruction in the immediate neighbourhood of places of public resort and when the streets may be thronged or obstructed. The civil law of trespass has also been used to obtain injunctions against demonstrators protesting against the motorway through Twyford Down. On the other hand the civil law of assault and wrongful arrest has been used by protesters to recover damages against the police for their conduct at demonstrations. This can be the most effective vindication of the right to protest peacefully.

THE HUMAN RIGHTS ACT 1998

The Human Rights Act 1998 has been hailed as the biggest change in U.K. law since 1688. This may be slightly misleading as the Act does not affect the sovereignty of Parliament, the fundamental principle of the constitution embodied in the Bill of Rights 1688. It does, however, greatly increase the power of the judiciary when interpreting legislation and thus profoundly affects the balance of power between Parliament and the courts.

Britain was the first country to ratify the European Convention on Human Rights (ECHR) in 1951 and individuals have been able to petition against the U.K. government for infringement of their rights under the Convention since 1966. More petitions have been brought against the U.K. and more have been upheld than against any other signatory, which allows individual petitions, except Italy. The delay involved in bringing such actions in the European Court of Human Rights in Strasbourg is on average five years and costs an average of £30,000.

Though U.K. governments have been meticulous in complying with the judgments of the Strasbourg court (even though this might be only to the minimum extent required to satisfy the judgment), the rights under the Convention were not enforceable in British courts, as they were in the courts of all the other countries who were parties to the Convention. However, the rights were increasingly being incorporated into English law by the back door. This was achieved firstly, through the common law by resorting to the Convention where the law was uncertain or by declaring that English law was the same as the right set out in the Convention. This technique was used particularly in cases concerned with freedom of speech, such as the *Spycatcher* case (1988), *Derbyshire County Council v. Times Newspapers Ltd.* (1993) and *Rantzen v. Mirror Group Newspapers Ltd.* (1993). However, as *Malone* (1979) (see above) has shown, the courts could not create new legal rights based on the Convention.

Secondly, the rule of statutory interpretation, that a statute or subordinate legislation should be construed where reasonably possible so as to be consistent with the international obligations of the U.K., meant that in cases of ambiguity the Convention could be called in aid. It was a matter for the courts to decide what constituted an ambiguity and in *R. v. Secretary of State for the Home Department ex parte Brind* (1991) the court refused to hold that the Home Secretary must conform to Article 10 of the Convention, which embodies the right to freedom of expression, when exercising his broad discretionary power to give a directive about broadcasting interviews with terrorists. Where the statutory provisions were found to be clear, the Convention could not be applied.

The Human Rights Act 1998 has not changed the position as radically as the rhetoric suggests. Unlike the European Communities Act 1972, the Act does not override the sovereignty of Parliament nor does it incorporate the Convention into English law. This was made clear during debates on the Bill in the House of Lords, when Lord Simon introduced an amendment to this effect, which was rejected and opposed by the Lord Chancellor as inconsistent with the key provision of the Act, section 3 (H.L. Deb., vol. 583, col. 507, November 18, 1997).

This central section 3 is a rule of interpretation, "So far as it is possible to do so, primary legislation and subordinate legislation must be read and given effect in a way which is compatible with the Convention rights". This section applies to primary and subordinate legislation whenever enacted and primary legislation is defined to include a prerogative Order in Council (see above, chapter 3). Section 3 further provides that incompatibility does not affect the validity or continuing operation of primary legislation. Thus the Human Rights Act does not affect the validity of an Act, which is incompatible with the Convention, whether it was passed before or after October 2, 2000, when the Human Rights Act 1998 came into force. It does, however, alter the normal rule of statutory interpretation that a later Act impliedly repeals an earlier Act to the extent that it is inconsistent. Lord Simon made several unsuccessful attempts in the House of Lords to reinstate this rule by amending the Bill. Paradoxically, the Human Rights Act does not breach the sovereignty of Parliament by binding future Parliaments but negates the corollary of the sovereignty of Parliament that a later Act impliedly repeals an earlier Act which is inconsistent with it.

To what extent does section 3 change the pre-existing rule of interpreting legislation consistent with the international obligations of the U.K.? According to the White Paper, which was published simultaneously with the Act, the provision goes far beyond the existing rule, which applied only in the case of ambiguity, whereas under the Act, "the courts will be required to interpret legislation so as to uphold the Convention rights unless the legislation itself is so clearly incompatible with the Convention that it is impossible to do so" (Cm 3782, para. 2.7). The way in which the courts are applying this provision will be illustrated below.

Where the court finds that primary legislation is incompatible with the Convention rights (set out in Schedule I), it may make a declaration of incompatibility. Where this is being considered, the court must give notice to the government and a minister is entitled to be joined as a party to the proceedings (section 5). The first case where this has been done involved the Consumer Credit Act 1974 and its provisions in relation to a loan agreement with a pawnbroker (see below). Only the High Court and superior courts can make such a declaration, which does not bind the parties in the case or affect the validity of the provision (section 4) but it does bring pressure on the government to take remedial action. The Act (section 10) provides a fast-track procedure to amend the incompatible legislation by subordinate legislation, in effect a Henry VIII clause (see, above chapter 3). As a result of amendments made during the passage of the Bill through Parliament, this procedure can only be used in the last resort where the minister considers there are compelling reasons. The procedure for such remedial orders was modelled on the two-stage procedure for deregulation orders (Schedule 2) and a Joint Committee of the Lords and Commons has been set up to scrutinise such orders at both stages and report its recommendations to each House. Where there are no compelling reasons to use the fast-track procedure, the government will have to use primary legislation to amend the incompatible statute, though it may, of course, decide to leave the offending Act intact. This may expose it to proceedings in the European Court of Human Rights and if these are successful there will be the obligation under the Convention to comply with the judgment.

A court can strike down subordinate legislation which it holds incompatible with Convention rights unless the Act under which it is made prevents the removal of the incompatibility, when the same procedure has to be used as for primary legislation.

To ensure the compatibility of legislation passed after the Human Rights Act 1998 with the Convention rights, each Act must be accompanied by a statement from the minister in charge of the Bill declaring that in his view it is compatible or, if this is not possible, that the Bill should nevertheless proceed (section 19). The minister will be expected to explain his reasons for this decision in the course of debates on the Bill but there are no provisions in the Human Rights Act 1998 for giving reasons in his statement on the Bill. As we have seen in this chapter, several Acts were passed in anticipation of the Human Rights Act coming into force to ensure compliance of existing legislation with the Convention rights. The government has also agreed to make a statement of compliance with the Convention rights in relation to subordinate legislation which is subject to approval by both Houses or which amends primary legislation (H.L. Deb., vol. 608, Col. 484, January 10, 2000).

However, the Human Rights Act does not only affect legislation. It also applies to the courts and, therefore, the common law which must comply with the Convention rights. Again, as we saw, the courts have anticipated the coming into force of the Act in certain areas. The courts are brought within the provisions of the Act by being defined as public authorities which are prohibited from acting in a way which is incompatible with the Convention rights (section 6). The Act does not list public authorities which are bound by the Act but defines them as persons, certain of whose functions are functions of a public nature (section 6(3c)). It will be left to the courts to interpret this provision. Where a person claims that a public authority has acted unlawfully, that is in contravention of Convention rights, he can, if he is a victim of that act bring proceedings against the authority (section 7). These may be for judicial review or an action for damages. In the latter case the court must take into account the principles applied by the European Court of Human Rights in relation to the award of damages. This Court awarded over £300,000 to four homosexuals who were dismissed from the armed forces. The judgments of the European Court must also be taken into account by a court determining any question in connection with a Convention right (section 2).

Two issues were particularly controversial during the passage of the Bill and led to two new clauses being inserted. They were concerned with the extent to which the churches and the press would be affected by the Bill. The churches were worried about conflict between the freedom to practise one's religion (Article 9) and other Convention rights such as freedom from discrimination (Article 14). The press were worried about the creation of a law of privacy as a result of Article 8 (right to privacy). Though the press are not public authorities as defined by the Act, they were afraid that the courts would be able to adapt the existing common law so as to fashion a right of privacy by reference to Article 8. They were placated by a new clause (section 12) which makes the court have particular regard to the importance of the right to freedom of expression and which makes it very difficult to obtain an injunction to restrain a publication before trial. The churches were placated by a new clause (section 13) making the court have particular regard to the importance of the Convention right to freedom of thought, conscience and religion when determining any question arising under the Act which might affect the exercise by a religious organisation of that right. These controversies show the conflicts which can arise between different Convention rights and that the Act can extend to the actions of private persons as well as public authorities.

Private individuals unlike public authorities cannot be sued for damages under the Act for acting in a way which is incompatible with the Convention rights but, as we saw, the common law has to be interpreted in conformity with these rights and this will affect actions between individuals. Similarly, any case involving the interpretation of legislation can raise the issue of whether the Act is compatible with the Convention rights. Thus the Human Rights Act will profoundly affect relationships between individuals as well as between citizens and the state.

The first case under the Human Rights Act where the court has considered making a declaration of incompatibility of provisions of an Act with the Convention rights and has notified the minister to that effect, concerns the Consumer Credit Act 1974. A loan agreement with a pawnbroking firm was held unenforceable under the Act but the Court of Appeal were concerned that the pawnbrokers had been denied a fair hearing (contrary to Article 6 of the Convention) under the Act because it made the agreement automatically unenforceable and that they had also been deprived of their property under Article 1 of Protocol 1 (*Wilson v. First County Trust Ltd*, 2001). The Court later made a declaration of incompatibility (*Wilson v. First County Trust Ltd (No2)*, 2001). The framers of the European Convention on Human Rights could not have foreseen that pawnbrokers might be the first beneficiaries of the Human Rights Act embodying the Convention.

Equally startling was the first important declaration of incompatibility which was made relating to planning law. It was held that, where the Secretary of State calls in a planning application for his own determination or decides a planning appeal himself instead of delegating it to an inspector (particularly where the government has a financial interest in the case) or where he confirms his own draft highway or compulsory purchase order, there is a breach of the right to a fair hearing under Article 6. The court said, "What is objectionable in terms of Article 6 is that he (the Secretary of State) should be the judge in his own cause where his policy is in play. In other words he cannot be both policy maker and decision taker" (para. 86). It would be different if the decision was taken by an inspector. The court was aware that its decision would have far reaching consequences and it was revesed on appeal to the House of Lords who held that the availability of judicial review of the Secretary of State's decision was sufficient to comply with Article 6 (*R (Alconbury Developments Ltd) v. Secretary of State for the Environment, Transport and the Regions*, 2001).

The courts can avoid making a declaration of incompatibility, which leaves the last word with Parliament, if they can interpret legislation so as to avoid it breaching Convention rights. This was the route taken by the Court of Appeal with respect to the Crime (Sentences) Act 1997 which provided for an automatic life sentence for a second serious offence unless there were exceptional circumstances. The court interpreted exceptional circumstances in a broad way so as in effect to restore the discretion which judges had before the Act was passed, *R. v. Offen*, (2001)). Under the Road Traffic Act 1988 motorists are required by law to tell the police who was driving their car. This was held by a Scottish court to breach the right against self-incrimination which is an ingredient of the right to a fair trial under Article 6. This case was, however, reversed by the Privy Council who held that the right against self-incrimination was not an absolute right and had to be balanced against the clear public interest in the enforcement of road traffic legislation (*Brown v. Stott* 2001),

In *McCartan Turkington Breen v. Times Newspapers Ltd.* (2000), a case heard by the House of Lords on the day after the Human Rights Act came into force, the court declined the invitation of counsel for the defendant newspaper to use section 3 of the Act to interpret the Defamation Act (Northern Ireland) 1955. The issue was whether the newspaper had a defence under the 1955 Act to defamation when reporting a defamatory statement about the plaintiff at a press conference to which they were invited. This depended on whether the press conference was a public meeting within the meaning of the Act. The House of Lords, overruling the lower courts, held that the press conference was a public meeting by using the ordinary principles of statutory interpretation. In the words of Lord Steyn these had to "be considered in the light of the legal norms of the contemporary legal system. And freedom of expression is a basic norm of our constitution" (p. 1686). He referred to previous cases such as *Reynolds v. Times Newspapers Ltd.* (1999) and *R. v. Secretary of State for the Home Department ex parte Simms* (2000), where this right had been asserted prior to the coming into force of the Human Rights Act. Lord Bingham stressed that, "The proper functioning of a modern participatory democracy requires that the media be free ... and the need for any restriction on that freedom to be proportionate and no more than is necessary to promote the legitimate object of the restriction" (pp. 1679–80). This mirrors the interpretation of Article 10 of the Convention which has been incorporated into English law without resort to the Human Rights Act. It is a technique which predates the Act coming into force but was here used in preference to applying the Act.

At this early stage of the Human Rights Act it seems that the courts are feeling their way, not using the Act where it is not necessary to reach the desired result and not resorting to a declaration of incompatibility where interpretation of legislation can make it compatible with the Convention rights. In Scotland where since May 1999, when devolution came into effect, both the Scottish Parliament and members of the Scottish Executive had to comply with the Convention rights, only about 16 out of 600 challenges have been successful (*The Guardian*, October 4, 2000). It is too early to predict the impact that the Human Rights Act will have but, judging by the number of times the issue has been raised in the short time since the Act was passed, it seems likely that there will be few human rights free zones. Whether or not challenges based on the Act are successful will be decided by the courts and there can be no doubt that the balance of power between the courts and Parliament and the government has been tipped heavily in favour of the courts, even though Parliament and, therefore, in effect the government, retains the final say. In practice this power is likely to be used rarely. The uncertainty in the law which the Act inevitably creates may be short-lived but the increase in the power of the courts can be characterised without too much exaggeration as the biggest change in U.K. law in more than 300 years.

CONCLUSION

"It may be that the era of pure representative democracy is slowly coming to an end" Mr Peter Mandelson M.P.

March 1998

In the last edition of this book the fear was expressed that the U.K. was becoming a one-party state where the party in government had been re-elected four times and the outlook for constitutional reform was bleak. Since then there has happened not only the election and re-election of a new government, with a large majority, but a plethora of constitutional reforms. The question is whether the state of the British constitution and its democratic institutions is now healthier than before.

In some areas the trends which were marked under the last government have continued and even been accentuated under the new one. The movement towards Prime Ministerial government rather than Cabinet government reached new heights. It can be summed up in the quip that Mr Blair is no longer primus inter pares (first among equals) but primus. Cabinet meetings have become a formality and key decisions are increasingly taken not even in Cabinet committees but in bilateral meetings between the Prime Minister and another Minister. The key decision to devolve power to the Bank of England to fix interest rates was, for example, decided by the Chancellor and the Prime Minister — members of the Cabinet were informed by telephone. The Code of Conduct for Ministers (Cabinet Office, 1997) requires the Prime Minister's approval in almost every paragraph.

One of the first acts of the new government was to strengthen the Prime Minister's office in Downing Street by trebling the number of political appointments. A special Civil Service Order in Council had to be made to allow two such appointees to have executive powers over civil servants. The number of special advisers to ministers has also doubled and the government has agreed to an upper limit to be fixed for the number of special advisers when legislation is introduced to put the civil service on a statutory footing (Cm 4817, 2000). This has not so far been a priority for this government any more than for its predecessors. More ominous for the politicisation of the civil service has been the appointment of former political advisers to senior civil service posts, even though these have to pass through the civil service appointments procedure. Most pervasive is the emphasis on modernisation which is a continuation of the previous government's drive for efficiency by importing management practices and a business rather than a public service ethos. This has not only resulted in civil servants being the most demoralised employees in the country (*The Guardian*, October 23, 2000) it has also led to more maladministration through cost-cutting, as has been noted by the Ombudsman.

The concentration on efficiency at the expense of fairness in the realm of tribunals and public inquiries has also been continued by this government. The Council on Tribunals has fought some vigorous rearguard actions against the streamlining of both these mechanisms for decision-making with some limited success but the bandwagon of modernisation rolls on inexorably. The price paid for efficiency in terms of fairness and equity are incalculable.

The fulcrum of a parliamentary democracy is the balance of power between the government and Parliament. The name of the game since 1997 has once more been modernisation with the setting up of a Modernisation Committee in the House of Commons and reform of the House of Lords. The changes which have been made as a result in the procedures of the House of Commons have in the main shifted the balance of power even further in favour of the government. Paradoxically, this has not been true of the reform of the House of Lords, which has assumed a new legitimacy, an unintended consequence of reform. Richard Shepherd M.P. has gone so far as to say that the Lords have become the working part of our constitution and the House of Commons the dignified (*i.e.* non-working) part (H.C. Deb., vol. 356, col. 191, November 7, 2000).

It may be hyperbole to say that the House of Commons is in crisis but there is undoubtedly a deep malaise felt on both sides of the House and in particular by backbenchers. There is an identity crisis as to whether an M.P.'s main function is to represent his party or to hold the government to account and whether his main work lies in the House or in his constituency. These conflicts were highlighted in debates on two procedural reforms. The first (H.C. Deb., vol. 356, col. 209, November 7, 2000) was to approve for one session of Parliament a procedure which sets a framework for programming, *i.e.* setting a time table for Bills immediately after

Second Reading. Though the Opposition and backbenchers will be involved in determining how debates on the Bill will be structured, they will be deprived of the weapon of delay which was a lever for negotiation about the passing of the Bill. There can be little doubt that the government has more to gain from the reform than the Opposition or backbenchers.

Another procedural change which was approved at the same time, as an experiment for one session of Parliament, was to postpone voting on certain issues after 10 p.m. to a specific time on the following Wednesday. This caused much controversy as it separates the debate on an issue from the decision on it through a vote. Delegated legislation is one of the areas where the vote will be deferred, making parliamentary control even more of a formality than at present. This procedural change is one of a number which make the sitting hours of the House more "family-friendly" by preventing voting after 10 p.m. and include starting and finishing the parliamentary day three hours earlier on Thursday. These reforms, which still leave the parliamentary sitting hours very different from a normal working day, have been much influenced by the debate about whether the prime function of M.P.s is centred in the House of Commons or in their constituencies.

The conflict between an M.P.s function as a representative of his party and as a representative of the people elected to hold the government to account was at the centre of the second debate on the reports of the Liaison Committee (*supra*, chapter 2) designed to make the Departmental Select Committees more independent of the government and shift the balance of power between Parliament and the Executive in favour of Parliament (H.C. Deb., Vol. 356, col. 473, November 9, 2000). In stark contrast to the debate on time tabling of legislation, no procedural changes were put before the House for approval. The Leader of the House thought that too little account was taken in the House of the role of political parties and accused the Liaison Committee of wanting Select Committees to substitute their judgments for that of the government. One Opposition M.P. thought that her speech would have pleased Charles I. The debate again illustrated modernisation as a euphemism for stream lining rather than reform, though some changes, such as pre-legislative scrutiny of Bills by Select Committees, have improved the legislative process, but this procedure has been used for only 12 Bills so far.

The same criticism can be made of the modernisation of local government which has been driven by a quest for efficiency rather than strengthening local democracy. The government's attitude to local government, where it has tightened some central controls and relaxed others, also illustrates a fundamental paradox at the heart of its constitutional reforms, some of which further centralise power in the Prime Minister and in the government *vis-à-vis* Parliament, whereas others devolve power away from central government to an unprecedented extent.

Nowhere is this more apparent than in devolution to Scotland and Wales and the creation of the Greater London Authority. The clumsy attempts to retain political control in these areas by influencing the choice of the First Minister in Wales and the London Mayor misfired. The fall-out from the creation of these alternative centres of power is only gradually becoming apparent and may shake the United Kingdom to its foundations. One solution points towards devolution to the regions as well as the countries of the United Kingdom but this remains unfinished business as does the fundamental reform of the House of Lords. These loose ends illustrate the lack of coherence in the constitutional reforms undertaken by the government. They have been aimed at specific problems and been driven more by political expediency than by a coherent constitutional philosophy.

The most far-reaching constitutional reform is the Human Rights Act 1998, which delegates wide powers to the judiciary within the formal limits of the sovereignty of Parliament. The effects of this reform are as yet incalculable but there can be no doubt that it has shifted the balance of power between Parliament and, therefore, the Executive and the judiciary in favour of the latter. This does raise fundamental issues about the health of our democracy. The power to control the government is effectively passing from Parliament to the courts. This marks an important constitutional shift and implies a lack of confidence in representative democracy.

This is illustrated in another way by the government's use of various forms of direct democracy such as a people's panel, citizens' juries, focus groups and telephone surveys. At the same time citizens are showing increasing apathy to vote at elections. Turn-out is falling for elections at all levels, local (about 30 per cent), national (about 59 per cent) and European. The latest European elections in 1999 reached a record low turn-out of 23 per cent, which was not a good advertisement for the system of proportional representation under which they were held for the first time. Though different forms of proportional representation are now used for devolved Parliaments and assemblies in Scotland, Wales, Northern Ireland and for the Greater London

Authority, there is silence on this issue so far as the U.K. Parliament is concerned. The Jenkins Commission report (*supra*, chapter 1) has been put on ice and the 2001 Labour manifesto commits the government to no more than a review of this issue. This is another item of unfinished constitutional reform.

The choice of a voting system for the U.K. Parliament goes to the heart of Britain's representative democracy. The present system normally delivers an overall majority for one party and, therefore, stable governments. But as Tony Wright M.P. said recently, "strong government can be defended only if it is matched by strong accountability". He then continued, "The Government are taking many admirable measures to insert new checks and balances into our political system, but the area where they have not done that — and they have to do it — is Parliament itself" (H.C. Deb., vol. 356, col. 512, November 9, 2000). This is the gaping hole at the heart of constitutional reform. It will not be filled unless M.P.s rise above party and act as representatives holding the government to account. Otherwise Mr. Mandelson's chilling prophesy about the end of representative democracy may become reality sooner rather than later. Not only have the voters lost faith in politicians but they seem to have lost faith in themselves.

The first successful revolt since 1997 by backbenchers against the government whips over the sacking of two independent-minded chairman of select committees, which occurred on July 16, 2001, offers a glimmer of hope.

BIBLIOGRAPHY

Bagehot,W. (1963) *The English Constitution*, London: Fontana.

Baker, D., Gamble, A. and Ludlam, S. (1993) 'Whips or scorpions? The Maastricht Vote and the Conservative Party', *Parliamentary Affairs*, p. 151.

Bell, K. (1975) *Research Study on Supplementary Benefit Appeal Tribunals*, London: HMSO.

Benn, A. (1980) 'The case for the Constitutional Premiership', *Parliamentary Affairs*, p. 7.

Lord Boyle (1980) 'Ministers and the Administrative Process', *Public Administration*, p. 1.

Brown, A. (2000) 'Designing the Scottish Parliament', *Parliamentary Affairs*, p. 542.

Dicey, A. V. (1939) *Law of the Constitution*, London: Macmillan.

Doig, A. (1993) 'The double whammy: the resignation of David Mellor, MP', *Parliamentary Affairs*, p. 167.

Finer, S.E. (1956) 'Individual responsibility of ministers', *Public Administration*, p. 377.

Ganz, G. (1974) *Administrative Procedures*, London: Sweet and Maxwell.

Ganz, G. (1990) 'Recent developments in the use of guillotine motions', *Public Law*, p. 496.

Genn, H. (1993) 'Tribunals and informal justice', *Modern Law Review*, p. 393.

Lord Hailsham (1976) 'Elective Dictatorship', *Listener*, October, 21.

Hansard Society (1992) *Making the Law: Report of the Hansard Society Commission on the Legislative Process*, London: The Hansard Society.

Harlow, C. and Rawlings, R. (1997) *Law and Administration*, London: Weidenfeld and Nicolson.

National Economic Development Office (1976) *A Study of UK Nationalised Industries*, London: HMSO.

Norton, P. (1982) *The Constitution in Flux*, Oxford: Martin Robertson.

Ryle, M. and Richards, P. G. (1988) *The Communs under Scrutiny*, 3rd edition, London: Routledge.

Walker, D. (1990) 'Enter the regulators', *Parliamentary Affairs*, p. 149.

Wass, Sir D. (1983) *The Reith Lectures*, London: BBC.

Zander, M. (1990) *The Police and Criminal Evidence Act 1984*, 2nd edition, London: Sweet and Maxwell.

Zander, M. (1999) *The State of Justice: 1999 Hamlyn Lectures*, London: Sweet and Maxwell.

TABLE OF CASES

TABLE OF STATUTES

INDEX